Managing Data
in Motion

T0383269

Managing Data in Motion

Data Integration Best Practice Techniques and Technologies

April Reeve

AMSTERDAM • BOSTON • HEIDELBERG • LONDON
NEW YORK • OXFORD • PARIS • SAN DIEGO
SAN FRANCISCO • SINGAPORE • SYDNEY • TOKYO

Morgan Kaufmann is an imprint of Elsevier

Acquiring Editor: Andrea Dierna
Development Editor: Heather Scherer
Project Manager: Mohanambal Natarajan
Designer: Russell Purdy

Morgan Kaufmann is an imprint of Elsevier
225 Wyman Street, Waltham, MA 02451, USA

Copyright © 2013 Elsevier Inc. All rights reserved.

No part of this publication may be reproduced or transmitted in any form or by any means, electronic or mechanical, including photocopying, recording, or any information storage and retrieval system, without permission in writing from the publisher. Details on how to seek permission, further information about the Publisher's permissions policies and our arrangements with organizations such as the Copyright Clearance Center and the Copyright Licensing Agency, can be found at our website: www.elsevier.com/permissions.

This book and the individual contributions contained in it are protected under copyright by the Publisher (other than as may be noted herein).

Notices
Knowledge and best practice in this field are constantly changing. As new research and experience broaden our understanding, changes in research methods or professional practices, may become necessary. Practitioners and researchers must always rely on their own experience and knowledge in evaluating and using any information or methods described herein. In using such information or methods they should be mindful of their own safety and the safety of others, including parties for whom they have a professional responsibility.

To the fullest extent of the law, neither the Publisher nor the authors, contributors, or editors, assume any liability for any injury and/or damage to persons or property as a matter of products liability, negligence or otherwise, or from any use or operation of any methods, products, instructions, or ideas contained in the material herein.

Library of Congress Cataloging-in-Publication Data
Application submitted

British Library Cataloguing-in-Publication Data
A catalogue record for this book is available from the British Library

ISBN: 978-0-12-397167-8

For information on all MK publications
visit our website at *www.mkp.com*

Printed and bound by CPI Group (UK) Ltd, Croydon, CR0 4YY
Transferred to digital print 2012

Working together to grow
libraries in developing countries

www.elsevier.com | www.bookaid.org | www.sabre.org

ELSEVIER   BOOK AID
                International   Sabre Foundation

For my sons

Henry
*who knows everything and, although he hasn't figured out exactly
what I do for a living, advised me to "put words on paper"*

and

David
*who is so talented, so much fun to be with, and always willing
to go with me to Disney.*

Contents

Foreword

Data integration has been the information systems profession's most enduring challenge.

It is almost four decades since Richard Nolan nominated data administration as the penultimate stage of his data processing maturity model, recognizing that the development of applications to support business processes would, unless properly managed, create masses of duplicated and uncoordinated data.

In the early days of database technology, some of us had a dream that we could achieve Nolan's objective by building all of our organizations' databases in a coordinated manner to eliminate data duplication: "Capture data once, store it in one place, and make it available to everyone who needs it" was the mantra.

Decentralized computing, packaged software, and plain old self-interest put an end to that dream, but in many organizations the underlying ideas lived on in the form of data management initiatives based on planning and coordination of databases—notably in the form of enterprise data models. Their success was limited, and organizations turned to tactical solutions to solve the most pressing problems. They built interfaces to transfer data between applications rather than capturing it multiple times, and they pulled it together for reporting purposes in what became data warehouses and marts. This pragmatic approach embodied a willingness to accept duplicated data as a given that was not attractive to the purists.

The tension between a strategic, organization-wide approach based on the disposition of data and after-the-fact spot solutions remains today. But the scale of the problem has grown beyond anything envisaged in the 1970s.

We have witnessed extraordinary advances in computing power, storage technology, and development tools. Information technology has become ubiquitous in business and government, and even midsized organizations count their applications in the thousands and their data in petabytes. But each new application, each new *solution*, adds to the proliferation of data. Increasingly, these solutions are "off the shelf," offering the buyer little say in the database design and how it overlaps with existing and future purchases.

Not only has the number of applications exploded, but the complexity of the data within them is worlds away from the simple structures of early files and databases. The Internet and smartphones generate enormous volumes of less structured data, "data" embraces documents, audio and video, and cloud computing both extends the boundary of the organization's data and further facilitates acquisition of new applications.

The need for data integration has grown proportionately—or more correctly, *disproportionately*, as the number of possible interfaces between systems increases exponentially. What was once an opportunistic activity is becoming, in many organizations, the focus of their systems' development efforts.

The last decade has seen important advances in tools to support data integration through messaging and virtualization. This book fills a vital gap in providing an overview of this technology in a form that is accessible to nonspecialists: planners, managers, and developers. April Reeve brings a rare combination of business perspective and detailed knowledge from many years of designing, implementing, and operating applications for organizations as an IT technician, manager and, more recently, a consultant using the technologies in a variety of different environments.

Perhaps the most important audience will be data managers, in particular those who have stuck resolutely to the static data management model and its associated tools. As the management of data in motion comes to represent an increasing proportion of the information technology budget, it demands strategic attention, and data managers, with their organization-wide remit, are ideally placed to take responsibility. The techniques in this book now form the mainstream of data integration thinking and represent the current best hope of achieving the data administration goals Nolan articulated so long ago.

—Graeme Simsion

Acknowledgements

First of all, I want to acknowledge the contribution of my husband, Tom Reeve, who said I had to acknowledge him for making me dinner. During the course of writing this book he made me dinner hundreds of times. Additionally, he put up with my constant mantra that "I have to write" instead of doing so many other things such as exercising or cleaning the house.

Of course I want to acknowledge the generosity of time and effort from all the data management experts that gave me interviews to use in this book:

- Let me start with David Allen who was my co-presenter at the tutorial we gave on this subject at the EDW conference in Chicago in 2011 and teaches me something fascinating about XML and JSON every time I see him, without him even knowing he is doing it.
- Krish Krishnan provided an abundance of information on his experience with data integration in data warehousing and set a wonderfully high standard for the expert interviews.
- James Anderson jumped in quickly when I lost my previous data archiving expert and it turns out we used to work together and now we are reconnected again.
- It was a pleasure to reconnect also with Adrienne Tannenbaum and get her perspective on metadata and data integration.
- I've always said that the more experienced we are the more we hate our tools, because we know the limitations, and it was great to get Dave Linthicum to look back on some of his experiences with enterprise service buses and the times when he might have had a love/hate relationship with them.
- I was very excited to get an interview with Dagna Gaythorpe, with all her experience in data modeling and its challenges, who provided a practitioners view on canonical data modeling that I found surprisingly optimistic.
- William McKnight helped me to get a handle on Hadoop, which is a critical subject for a current book on data integration.
- I met John Haddad when we were both on a Big Data panel at EDW 2012 and he generously offered to help me with this book, which he did by reading and providing feedback on some of the early sections as well as a perfect interview on big data.
- Although Mike Ferguson couldn't provide an interview, attending his workshop did provide me with a great deal of my understanding of data virtualization, which is a core concept in big data integration.

Karl Glenn was one of the technical reviewers of the book and I appreciated his perspective and advice very much. It was amazing to discover someone who lived on another continent and yet shared much of my understanding and perspective regarding best practices with data integration.

And one last shout out for my editor, Andrea Dierna, who is amazingly calm in a crisis.

Biography

April Reeve has spent the last 25 years working as an enterprise architect and program manager for large multinational organizations, developing data strategies and managing development and operation of solutions. April is an expert in multiple data management disciplines including data conversion, data warehousing, business intelligence, master data management, data integration, and data governance. Currently, she is working for EMC^2 Consulting as an Advisory Consultant in the Enterprise Information Management practice.

Introduction

What this book is about and why it's necessary

Most organizations of middle to large size have hundreds or, more probably, thousands of applications, each with its own various databases and other data stores. Whether the data stores are from traditional technologies and database management systems, emerging technologies, or document management systems, it is critical to the usefulness of these applications to the organization that they share information between them. Developing and managing solutions for moving data between applications becomes an overwhelmingly complex problem unless addressed using a coordinated approach across an organization. This book describes a reasonable approach and architecture that enables managing the cacophony of interfaces in an application portfolio.

The focus of data management by information technology functions tends to be around the efficient management of data sitting in databases or "persistent" data that sits still. Since currently in most organizations applications are primarily purchased vendor solutions, managing the data that travels between systems, applications, data stores, and organizations— the "data in motion"— should be a central focus of information technology for any organization. Custom development in most organizations will continue to be more around the data traveling between applications than the development of new applications.

What the reader will learn

This book provides an overview of the different techniques, technologies, and best practices used to manage the passing of data between computer systems and integrating disparate data together in a large organization environment.

The reader will learn about best practice techniques for developing and managing data integration solutions for an organization and the set of tools, or architecture, that an organization should have to support a robust organizational data integration capability, broken down by the various types of data integration that are relevant: batch, real-time, or big data integration.

All should read Chapter 2 on "The Importance of Data Integration and the Natural Complexity of Data Interfaces" and Chapter 12 on "Data Integration Patterns and Hub and Spoke," which is key to turning the unmanageable complexity of interfaces in an organization into a data layer that can be reasonably managed. The information presented in these chapters is the basis for developing a financial justification for a data integration program in their organization.

Who should read this book

This book was written for five categories of people:

- Senior-level business and IT managers
- Enterprise data, application, and technical architects
- Data-related program and project managers, including those for data warehouses, master data management programs, data conversion and migration, and data archiving
- Data analysts, data modelers, database practitioners, and data integration programmers
- Data management students

This book contains references to various types of technology solutions to data integration problems, but does not require an extensive technical background for understanding. Senior Business and Information Technology Managers

Managing the cacophony of interactions and interfaces between the thousands of applications and databases in most organizations is one of the primary challenges associated with managing an IT portfolio. Senior-level managers, both those in information technology and those who need to understand the issues involving managing an application system portfolio, may be interested in an overview of the techniques, technologies, and best practices associated with managing the data traveling around their organization and to other organizations. This area of data management has previously been viewed almost exclusively of concern to only the very detailed technical areas of an organization. Besides the fact that managers should have an understanding of the main parts of their technology investments, significant gains in productivity are to be obtained through some simple architectural decision in data integration technology and management that no organization can afford to ignore. Enterprise Data, Application, and Technical Architects

Enterprise architects, especially those associated with data and application architecture but also those dealing in more technical components, should certainly have an understanding of the data integration solutions needed in an organization's technical portfolio and architectural planning. The data architecture of every organization should include layers supporting data security, business intelligence, database management, document management, and, certainly, data integration. Data-Related Program and Project Managers

Program and project managers in data warehousing, master data management, data conversion, data archiving, business intelligence, metadata, and so on, should have an understanding of the techniques for moving data between applications and integrating data into and out of data hubs.

Data analysts, data modelers, database practitioners, and data integration programmers

Many people are working on data integration projects as data analysts, programmers, or other titles, and performing all kinds of detailed functions such as ETL programmers, SOA architects, and data service modelers. A broader understanding of why certain functions are designed or performed the way they are and the neighboring and emerging technologies in this area can only help to improve their current effectiveness and future prospects. An understanding of how the work they are currently doing fits it to the broader framework of the organization's technology can help them focus on the most important goals of their work and to bring to light situations where things are not occurring as intended. Learning about some of the emerging technologies in this area can help to identify areas of possible interest and career development.

Data management students

In universities, information technology training tends to focus on programming and technology training. Database training focuses on creating new individual databases. In practice, organizations develop a few new databases, but mostly struggle to manage those already existing. The interaction of thousands of applications and data stores may be hard for a student to visualize. The set of techniques and technologies developed to solve the various data integration problems provides an important, wide base of understanding for a student to grasp.

How this book is organized

This book provides an overview of the different techniques, technologies, and best practices used to manage the passing of data between computer systems and integrating disparate data together in a large organization environment. Each section describes the architecture, or set of tools and technologies, needed to support the type of data integration capability specified in that section: batch, real-time, and big data integration. Also included in each section are interviews with experts in different technologies associated with data integration and case studies showcasing my own experiences.

Current practitioners in data integration may want to skip forward past the basic sections to the areas on data integration with which they are not yet familiar, such as Part IV on big data integration.

Most existing books in this area tend to focus on the implementation of specific technologies or solutions, but here is a broad inventory of data integration solutions, the various techniques, their benefits, and challenges.

Part 1: Introduction to data integration

This first section of the book focuses on the importance of achieving data integration in an organization's data management planning and making managing data in motion much more efficient.

Chapter 1: What is data integration?

This chapter presents an overview of the processes that collectively can be referred to as data integration: moving data, transforming data, migrating data from one application to another, pulling information together, and distributing processes out to data.

Chapter 2: The importance of data integration

This Chapter Presents the Reasons Why Data Integration Should Be an Important Topic for Managing Data in an Organization and Almost Every Organization Should Have a Data Integration Layer in Its IT Architecture.

Chapter 3: Types and complexity of data integration

This chapter presents an overview of the types of data integration, each of which is covered in detail in a separate section of the book: batch data integration, real-time data integration, and big data integration.

Chapter 4: The process of data integration development

This chapter deals with the standard development life cycle on data integration projects and the types of resources needed to be successful.

Part 2: Batch data integration

The second section of the book discusses data integration techniques and technologies associated with very large-volume data movement that have usually been with batch, or asynchronous data integration, used for activities such as data conversions and moving data into data warehouses.

Chapter 5: Introduction to batch data integration

This chapter describes the batch data integration capability.

Chapter 6: Extract, transformation, and load

This chapter describes the core data integration ETL process flow that is used for all types of data integration, and most especially for batch data integration.

Chapter 7: Data warehousing

This chapter provides a description of data warehousing and most especially how data is loaded into and extracted out of a data warehouse. There is also an interview with data warehousing expert Krish Krishnan on data warehousing and data integration.

Chapter 8: Data conversion

This chapter describes the process of data conversion, also known as data migration, and how data integration is integral to the data conversion process.

Chapter 9: Data archiving

This chapter focuses on the process of data archiving and the importance of data integration. It includes an interview with expert James Anderson on data archiving and data integration.

Chapter 10: Batch data integration architecture and metadata

This chapter outlines the tools necessary to implement a batch data integration capability for profiling, modeling, storing metadata, performing data movement, transformation, and scheduling. It includes an interview with metadata expert Adrienne Tannenbaum on metadata and data integration.

Part 3: Real-time data integration

The third section of the book discusses data integration best practices associated with real-time or synchronous data integration, used for passing information between interactive operational applications and systems.

Chapter 11: Introduction to real-time data integration

This chapter describes the real-time data integration capability.

Chapter 12: Data integration patterns

This chapter categorizes and describes the basic patterns used in real-time data integration, especially the critical "hub-and-spoke" approach to data interfaces.

Chapter 13: Core real-time data integration technologies

This chapter provides a brief description of the key technologies used in real-time data integration: ESB, SOA, XML, EAI, and EII. Included is an interview with XML expert M. David Allen on the importance of XML in real-time data integration and an interview with data integration expert David Linthicum on enterprise service buses.

Chapter 14: Data integration modeling

This chapter describes the critical area of data modeling in data integration, especially real-time data integration. Data-modeling expert Dagna Gaythorpe provides an interview on some of her experiences with canonical data modeling, integral to hub-and-spoke interface architecture.

Chapter 15: Master data management

This chapter describes the area of master data management and how data integration is intertwined and essential to its success.

Chapter 16: Data warehousing with real-time updates

This chapter provides a description of real-time updates in data warehousing. Data warehousing expert Krish Krishnan continues his interview on data warehousing and real-time data integration.

Chapter 17: Real-time data integration architecture and metadata

This chapter outlines the tools necessary to implement a real-time data integration capability for profiling, modeling, storing metadata, performing data movement, transformation, and event orchestration.

Part 4: Big data integration

The last section of the book is about data integration associated with emerging technologies such as cloud computing, visualization, massively parallel processing, and data virtualization.

Chapter 18: Introduction to big data integration

This chapter provides an introduction to the data integration capability with big data.

Chapter 19: Cloud architecture and data integration

This chapter provides a brief description of cloud architecture and the additional issues and concerns associated with integrating data from within and organization with data located in a cloud solution.

Chapter 20: Data virtualization

This chapter describes data virtualization, which is the technology central to big data integration.

Chapter 21: Big data integration

This chapter gives an overview of big data and then outlines the tools necessary to implement a real-time data integration capability.

Chapter 22: Conclusion to managing data in motion

This chapter concludes the presentation of data integration and summarizes the technical solutions required for implementing various data integration capabilities: batch data integration, real-time data integration, and big data integration.

Introduction to Data Integration

The Importance of Data Integration

The natural complexity of data interfaces

The average corporate computing environment is comprised of hundreds or even thousands of disparate and changing computer systems that have been built, purchased, and acquired. The data from these various systems needs to be integrated for reporting and analysis, shared for business transaction processing, and converted from one system format to another when old systems are replaced and new systems are acquired. Effectively managing the data passing between systems is a major challenge and a concern for every information technology organization.

Most data management focus is around data stored in structures such as databases and files, and a much smaller focus is on the data flowing between and around the data structures. Yet, management of the data interfaces in organizations is rapidly becoming a main concern for business and information technology (IT) management. As more systems are added to an organization's portfolio, the number and complexity of the interfaces between the systems grow dramatically, making management of those interfaces overwhelming.

Traditional interface development quickly leads to a level of complexity that is unmanageable. The number of interfaces between applications and systems may become an exponential factor of the number of systems. In practice, not every system needs to interface with every other, but there may be multiple interfaces between systems for different types of data or needs. For an organization with 100 applications, there may be something like 5000 interfaces. A portfolio of 1000 applications may provide half a million interfaces to manage.

An implementation of some data integration best practice techniques can make the management of an organization's interfaces much more reasonable

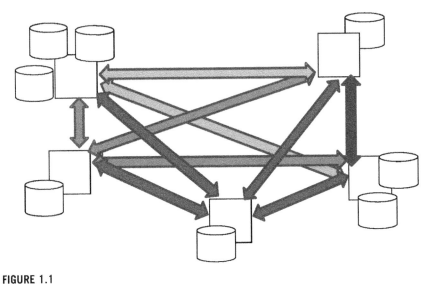

FIGURE 1.1

Point-to-Point Interface Complexity.

than the traditional "point to point" data integration solutions, as depicted in Figure 1.1, which generate this type of management challenge. An organization that develops interfaces without an enterprise data integration strategy can quickly find managing the vast numbers of interfaces that ensue impossible.

The rise of purchased vendor packages

It has been the general consensus for years that, in most cases, except for strategically differentiating applications, it is more cost effective to purchase packages and configure appropriately for the organization, thus sharing the cost of developing functionality, supporting new feature development, and detecting and resolving problems across the various organizations using the software. Another term for purchased package is COTS (Commercial Off the Shelf) software.

Since the vast majority of software applications being implemented at organizations now are purchased vendor packages, the work and process of integrating the specific portfolio of software being run in a particular organization is one of the few remaining custom development activities. Software vendors can develop systems in ways to support integration and interactions with the other systems in the portfolio, but the specific portfolio of systems requiring integration in an organization, and therefore the data integration solution, are unique to each organization.

Most additions to the application system portfolio are purchased packages, but packages invariably will contain their own definition of important master data structures, such as customer, product, and organization hierarchy. Since master

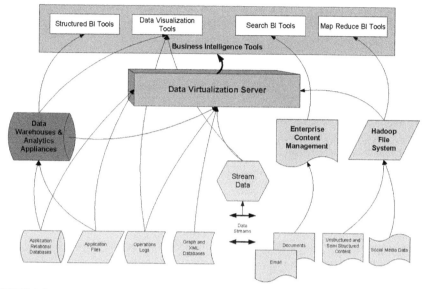

FIGURE 1.2

Big Data Architecture.

data will invariably exist in any custom applications as well as any other packages in the portfolio, it will be necessary to integrate the master data across the applications. Therefore, although the practice of purchasing application solutions rather than building custom makes the management and ongoing support of an application portfolio somewhat easier, it also makes the required integration of data across the application portfolio more complex than if all applications were custom developed and utilized common data structures.

Key enablement of big data and virtualization

In the emerging areas of big data, cloud processing, and data virtualization, critical components of the implementation of these technologies and solutions are data integration techniques.

With big data, it is frequently a better solution, rather than consolidating data prior to analysis, to leave the vast amounts and various types of data where they are and distribute the processing out to the data, that is, a parallel processing solution. When the results of the requests have acted on the distributed data, the results need to be consolidated and returned. Data integration is critical to big data solutions, but the solutions may be significantly different from traditional data integration. As depicted in Figure 1.2, the arrows indicate the existence of data integration solutions to transport and consolidate data between the various and sundry data structures.

Cloud architectures with the external and virtual server solutions, data replication, and need for fault-tolerant solutions rely on data integration solutions. Again, however, the implementation of data integration solutions in a cloud environment is very different from those in traditional data centers, but builds on the basic concepts developed over the last two decades in data integration.

Infrastructure and server virtualization is widely implemented in many organizations because of the flexibility in infrastructure management it allows. These solutions play nicely with some data integration solutions but require adjustments with others, such as enterprise service bus technology.

In-memory data structures and processing can provide performance improvements of multiple magnitudes and rely on many data integration techniques, but they need to be implemented in ways that leverage the strengths of in-memory processing capabilities.

The capabilities of data virtualization represent the culmination of more than two decades of experience with data integration and many thousands of hours fine tuning various data integration techniques and technologies. With all its benefits, data virtualization can be viewed as a breakthrough that stands upon the experience with the disciplines of data warehousing, business intelligence, and, most critically, data integration.

What Is Data Integration?

Data in motion

Planning the management of data in data stores is about "persistent" data that sits still. Managing the data that travels between systems, applications, data stores, and organizations—the "data in motion"—is central to the effectiveness of any organization and the primary subject of this book.

It shouldn't be news that available, trusted data is absolutely critical to the success of every organization. The processes of making the data "trusted" is the subject of data governance and data quality, but making the data "available"—getting the data to the right place, at the right time, and in the right format—is the subject of data integration.

The practice associated with managing data that travels between applications, data stores, systems, and organizations is traditionally called data integration (DAMA international, 2009). This terminology may be a little misleading to those who are not used to the term. *Data integration* intuitively sounds to be more about the consolidation of data, but it is the movement, not the persistence that is the focus. *Data interface* refers to an application written to implement the movement of data between systems.

Integrating into a common format—transforming data

Usually, the most complex and difficult part of integrating data is transforming data into a common format. Understanding the data to be combined and

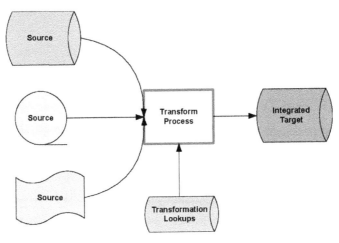

FIGURE 2.1

Transforming Data into a Common Format.

understanding (and possibly defining) the structure of the combined data requires both a technical and business understanding of the data and data structures in order to define how the data needs to be transformed.

In Figure 2.1, multiple sources of data of different formats are transformed into an integrated target data set. Many data transformations are accomplished simply by changing the technical format of the data, but frequently, as depicted in the diagram, additional information needs to be provided to look up how the source data should be transformed from one set of values to another.

Migrating data from one system to another

When an application in an organization is replaced, either by a new custom application or by a purchased package, data from the old system needs to be migrated to the new application. The new application may already be in production use and additional data is being added, or the application may not yet be in use and the data being added will populate empty data structures.

As shown in Figure 2.2, the data conversion process interacts with the source and target application systems to move and transform from the technical format needed by the source system to the format and structure needed by the target system. This is best practice, especially to allow a data update to be performed by the

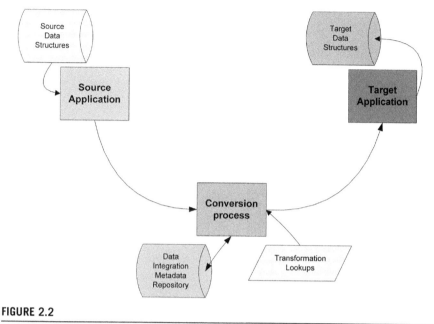

FIGURE 2.2

Migrating Data from One Application to Another.

owning application code rather than updating the target data structures directly. There are times, however, when the data migration process interacts directly with the source or target data structures instead of the application interfaces.

Moving data around the organization

Most organizations of middle to large size have hundreds or, more probably, thousands of applications, each with its own various databases and other data stores. Whether the data stores are from traditional technologies and database management systems, emerging technologies, or other types of structures such as documents, messages, or audio files, it is critical to the organization that these applications can share information between them. Independent, stand-alone applications that do not share data with the rest of the organization are becoming less and less useful.

The focus of information technology planning in most organizations tends to be around the efficient management of data in databases and other data stores. This may be because ownership of the spaces between the applications running in an organization may be unclear, and so somewhat ignored. Data integration

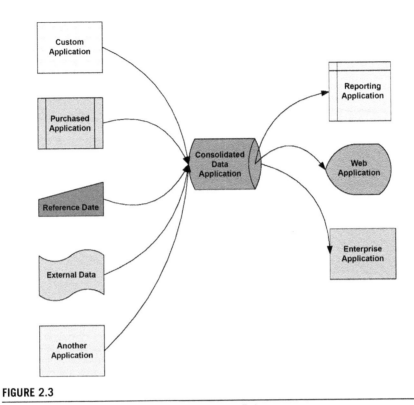

FIGURE 2.3

Moving Data into and out of Central Consolidation Points.

solutions have tended to be implemented as accompanying persistent data solutions such as data warehouses, master data management, business intelligence solutions, and metadata repositories.

Although traditional data interfaces were usually built between two systems "point to point," with one sending and another receiving data, most data integration requirements really involve multiple application systems that want to be informed real time of changes to data from multiple source application systems. Implementing all data interfaces as point to point solutions quickly becomes overwhelmingly complex and practically impossible for an organization to manage. As depicted in Figure 2.3, specific data management solutions have been designed to centralize data for particular uses to simplify and standardize data integration for an organization, such as data warehousing and master data management. Real-time data integration strategies and solutions now involve designs of data

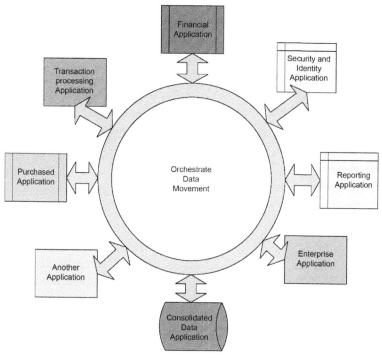

FIGURE 2.4

Moving Data around the Organization.

movement that are significantly more efficient than point to point as depicted in Figure 2.4.

Pulling information from unstructured data

In the past, most data integration projects involved almost exclusively data stored in databases. Now, it is imperative that organizations integrate their database (or structured) data with data in documents, e-mail, websites, social media, audio, and video files. The common term for data outside of databases is *unstructured data*. Integration of data of various types and formats usually involves use of the keys or tags (or metadata) associated with unstructured data that contains information relating the data to a customer, product, employee, or other piece of master data. By analyzing unstructured data containing text, it may be possible to

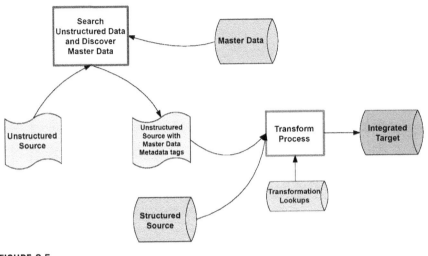

FIGURE 2.5

Pulling Information from Unstructured Data.

associate the unstructured data with a customer or product. Thus, an e-mail may contain references to customers or products that can be identified from the text and added as tags to the e-mail. A video may contain images of a customer that can be matched to the customer image, tagged, and linked to the customer information. Metadata and master data are important concepts that are used to integrate structured and unstructured data.

As shown in Figure 2.5, data found outside of databases, such as documents, e-mail, audio, and video files, can be searched for customers, products, employees, or other important master data references. Master data references are attached to the unstructured data as metadata tags that then can be used to integrate the data with other sources and types.

Moving process to data

In an age of huge expansion in the volume of data available to an organization (big data), sometimes it is more efficient to distribute processing to the multiple locations of the data rather than collecting data together (and thus duplicating) in order to process it. Big data solutions frequently approach data integration from a significantly different perspective than the traditional data integration solutions.

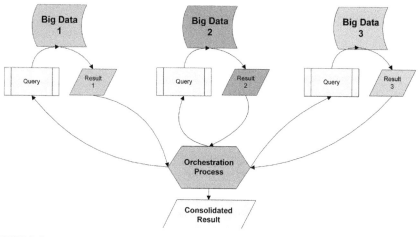

FIGURE 2.6

Moving Process to Data.

As shown in Figure 2.6, in some cases of working with very large volumes, it is more effective to move the process to the data and then consolidate the much smaller results.

Emerging big data solutions are mostly used by programmers and technologists or highly skilled specialists such as data scientists.

Types and Complexity of Data Integration

INFORMATION IN THIS CHAPTER

The differences and similarities in managing data in motion and persistent data

Data access and security management are primary concerns for both persistent and moving data. Persistent data security is usually managed in layers: physical, network, server, application, and at the data store. Data traveling between applications and organizations needs additional security to protect the data in transit from unauthorized access. Methods for securing data while in transit, using encryption at the sending point and decryption at the intended receiving point, are robust and complex areas of study with interesting histories involving spies and devices going back to the beginning of recorded history, none of which is a topic in this book.

Recovery from failures in processing is a critical subject for both persistent data processing and transient data processing. The techniques for recovery are very different but with some related approaches for the two methods. Actually, every technology and tool may have different methods for recovery that will make them appropriate for various business and technical solutions. The two things that are important to determine in choosing an appropriate solution are how much data can be allowed to be lost in a failure and how long the systems can be down before recovery must occur. The smaller the amount of data it is acceptable to lose and the smaller the amount of time of acceptable downtime, the more expensive the appropriate recovery solution. But the subject of business continuity and recovery from failure is also not a part of this book.

With persistent data, much of the concern is about the model or structure of the data being stored. In managing data in motion, the largest concern is how to associate, map, and transform data between different systems. There is an important part of the implementation of data integration solutions which does involve the modeling of the data in transit and the use of a central model of the data passing between applications; this is called canonical modeling.

Batch data integration

Batch data integration occurs when data to be transferred from a source to a target is grouped together and sent periodically, such as daily, weekly, or monthly.Most interfaces between systems in the past used to be in the form of passing a large file of data from one system to another on a periodic basis. The contents of the file would be records of consistent layout, and the sending and receiving application systems would agree to and understand the format. The passing of data between two systems whereby a sending system passes data to a target receiving system is called "point to point". The data file would be processed by the receiving system at some point in time, not necessarily instantaneously; thus the interface would be "asynchronous" because the sending system would not be waiting for an immediate confirmation before the transaction would be considered complete. The "batch" approach to data integration is still appropriate and effective for very large data interactions such as data conversions and loading data snapshots into data warehouses. This type of interface can be tuned to be extremely fast and is appropriate where very large volumes of data need to be loaded as quickly as possible. It is also described as "tightly coupled" because the format of the data file must be agreed to between the systems and can only change successfully if the two systems involved incorporate knowledge of the change simultaneously.

Tight coupling requires carefully managed orchestration of changes to multiple systems to be implemented at the same time in order for the interfaces not to "break," or stop working either correctly or at all. In managing large portfolios of application systems, it is preferable to have a looser coupling of system interfaces in order to allow changes to applications that don't immediately break other systems and don't require such careful coordination of simultaneous changes. Therefore, it is usually preferable that data integration solutions are "loosely coupled."

Real-time data integration

Interfaces that are necessary across systems immediately in order to complete a single business transaction are called "real-time" interfaces. Usually they would involve a much smaller amount of data being passed in the form of a "message." Most real-time interfaces are still point to point between a sending and receiving system and tightly coupled because the sending and receiving systems still have specific agreement as to the format, such that any change must be made to the two systems simultaneously.Real-time interfaces are usually called synchronous because the transaction will wait for the data interface to complete its processing in both the sending and receiving systems.

Best practices in real-time data integration solutions break away from the complexity problems of point-to-point and tightly coupled interface design. There are logical design solutions that can be implemented in various technologies. These technologies can be used to implement inefficient data integration as well, if the underlying design concerns are not understood.

Big data integration

The term "big data" indicates that there are large volumes of data, as well as data of various technologies and types. Taking into account the extra volumes and various formats, data integration of big data may involve distributing the processing of the data to be performed across the source data in parallel and only integrating the results, because consolidating the data first may take too much time and cost too much in extra storage space.

Integrating structured and unstructured data involves tying together common information between them, which is probably represented as master data or keys in structured data in databases and as metadata tags or embedded content in unstructured data.

Data virtualization

Data virtualization involves using various data integration techniques to consolidate data real-time from various sources and technologies, not just structured data. "Data warehousing" is a practice in data management whereby data is copied from various operational systems into a persistent data store in a consistent format to be used for analysis and reporting. The practice is used to do analysis across snapshots of historical data, among other things, which is difficult using active operational data. Even when the data required for analysis is only current data, the reporting and analysis architecture usually involves some persistent data store, such as a "data mart" because the real-time integration and harmonizing of data from various sources has previously been found to be too slow for real-time consumption. However, new data virtualization technologies make real-time data integration for analysis feasible, especially when used in conjunction with data warehousing. Emerging technologies using in-memory data stores and other virtualization approaches allow for very fast data integration solutions that do not have to rely on intermediate persistent data stores, such as data warehouses and data marts.

The Process of Data Integration Development

The data integration development life cycle

The life cycle for developing a new interface between systems is very similar to that of other data-related development disciplines. Critical to success is the analysis of the actual data on both the source and target sides of the proposed data movement. Also, although Figure 4.1 shows that the steps toward implementation and operation are sequential and distinct, they are actually more iterative and overlapping than depicted, with testing of assumptions and designs being performed as early as possible using analysis tools and prototypes.

Figure 4.1 depicts the data integration life cycle. The first part of the life cycle is the scoping of the project: high-level requirements, high-level design, data requirements, identification of sources and targets. The process starts with high-level requirements: What is the basic data movement requirement that needs to be met? It could be that customer data needs to be synchronized across the enterprise, some data from an external organization needs to be made available, additional data should be included in reports, social media data should be used for predictive analytics, or a myriad of other possible data movement requirements. Then, some basic concept of design is specified: Does this need to happen once a day in batch or real time? Is there a data integration platform in place ready for use, or is something additional needed? Another more detailed round of requirements and design should identify what data is needed and potential sources and targets of the data in question.

The next part of the data integration life cycle is frequently ignored: profiling. Because data integration is regarded as a technical discipline and because, rightfully, organizations are sensitive about giving access to production data, it may be difficult to analyze the data that currently resides in the data stores of potential

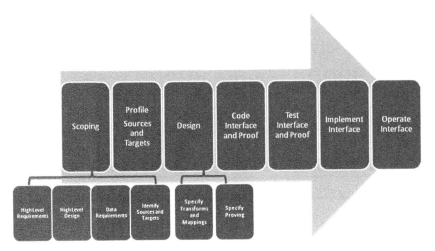

FIGURE 4.1

Data Integration Life Cycle.

source and target applications for the data interfaces. The step of profiling the actual data to be involved in the data integration is critical to successful development. Every data integration project discovers something in the actual data of the potential sources and targets that significantly affects the design of the solution, whether it is unexpected content, the lack of content, or poor quality data, or even that the data required doesn't actually exist where it was expected. Negotiation with data owners and data security groups should be continued until an acceptable solution is achieved that allows data profiling on the proposed source and target data.

All data integration solutions should include some proving process that is executed periodically while the data interface is in production to ensure that the data from the source applications have successfully been incorporated into the data structures of the target applications. Data proving should be done using an alternative means of extract to the data interface, such as running the same report on the source and target systems and compare the results. Proving is essential for data conversion projects but is important for all data integration.

Inclusion of business knowledge and expertise

Data integration has been viewed as a very technical practice within data management, wholly the domain of technologists, as opposed to the other extreme of data governance and data quality, which are almost wholly business process-oriented practices. However, effective data integration also requires a business understanding of the data being passed between systems.

Many applications and projects that rely on data integration (conversion, data warehousing, master data management) are subject to delays in implementation, not because of a lack of technological solutions but because of a lack of business knowledge and business involvement.

One of the core processes in data integration development, specifying the data transformations, must be reviewed and verified by someone with detailed business understanding of the data. Many tools can be used to try and deduce the relationships between data in various systems, either through similarities in the field names or an actual analysis of the data contents. Ultimately, however, these deductions are only educated guesses that must be verified by the actual business users of the data.

The real challenge is that some of the steps in the data project life cycle as depicted in Figure 4.1 cannot be easily segregated between steps to assign to a technical resource versus those to assign to a business resource. The requirements steps and the specific mappings and transformation rules must be completed by someone who understands both aspects of the data in question or by people from multiple groups working closely together. To define the mappings and transformations, for example, knowledge of both the physical implementation of the data and how that same data is actually used in business processes is necessary.

A technical resource might know, or can find out, that a particular field on a screen is mapped to a particular field in a data store that might or might not have a similar name. A business resource may know which field on the screen they want to extract for some purpose but may not know where that field is necessarily stored in the physical data structures. Profiling the candidate source data, once potential fields have been identified, will almost certainly highlight information about the actual data of which neither technical nor business resources were aware but will require both technical and business resources to understand the profile results. All this information will be necessary in order to specify the correct mapping and data transformation requirements for the source data.

Both technical and business knowledge of the source and target data are critical to the success of data integration projects, and this need for multiple resources from usually different functional areas to coordinate on all steps in the solution development life cycle is the most challenging aspect of data integration development.

Batch Data Integration

Introduction to Batch Data Integration

INFORMATION IN THIS CHAPTER

What is batch data integration?

Most interfaces between systems traditionally have been in the form of passing a large file of data from one system to another on a periodic basis, such as daily, weekly, or monthly. The contents of the file would be records of a consistent layout, and the format would be agreed to and understood between the sending and receiving application systems. This process is called batch mode because the data is "batched" into groups and sent periodically rather than individually in real time. This standard batch data integration process is depicted in Figure 5.1. The passing of data between two systems in which a sending system passes data to a target-receiving system is called point to point.

This "batch" approach to data integration is still appropriate and effective for very large data interactions such as data conversions and loading periodic snapshots into data warehouses. The data loading can be tuned to be extremely fast and is useful where very large volumes of data need to be loaded as quickly as possible. It is also described as "tightly coupled" because the systems must agree on the format of the data file, and the format can only change successfully if the two systems involved implement knowledge of the change simultaneously. Replacing either the sending or receiving system usually involves the need to rewrite the interface for the other system.

Data backup and recovery is not usually addressed under the subject of data integration, and it won't be covered in this book. Data backup and recovery is usually handled by specialized hardware and software utilities that are proprietary to the data structures in which the data is stored and tend to be highly optimized

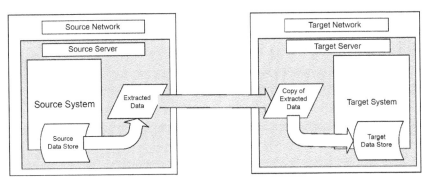

FIGURE 5.1

Extract, Transformation, and Load Data Flow.

and efficient. The subject is discussed by specific data structure and storage vendors and under the topic of business continuity.

Batch data integration life cycle

The batch data integration development life cycle is similar to other data-related projects but have a slightly different recommended life cycle from projects that are not data centric. Prior to the development of a batch data integration flow, or a batch data interface, the scope of the interface has to be defined regarding affected sources and targets with an initial concept of the attributes to be involved.

The scoping exercise involves high-level requirements and design in order to determine that batch data integration is an appropriate solution. An initial definition of the data to be involved in the interface is specified, including what attributes are required to be populated in the target and an educated guess as to what attributes would need to be extracted from the source or sources in order to determine the appropriate values of the target.

A highly recommended best practice critical to the success of building a data interface is to profile the actual data in the source and target data structures. Profiling actual production data is essential to understanding the way the target data should look and in which sources the appropriate attributes will be found. Basic profiling will involve understanding various aspects of what the data in question actually looks like, not just what has been documented or thought to be the case, including uniqueness, density (nulls or blanks), format, and valid values.

Specification of the required transformation of data from the source format to the target requires a combination of business and technical knowledge. People who are both business and technologically knowledgeable should review and

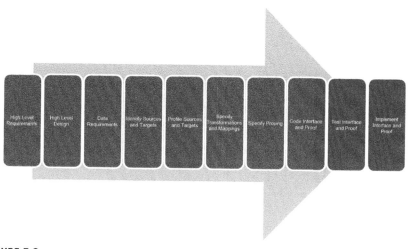

FIGURE 5.2

Batch Data Integration Life Cycle.

agree to the specified design of the data transformation based on high-level requirements and profiling results.

The development of a data interface should include some kind of data-proving process that runs periodically to check that the data from the source systems is in agreement with what has been passed to the target systems.

Figure 5.2 portrays a highly delineated series of steps. In practice, it is best to use an iterative, agile, or prototype approach to developing the data interface where the data movement is proven without a large amount of time or effort passing between design and test.

Extract, Transform, and Load

INFORMATION IN THIS CHAPTER

What is ETL?

The core function of data integration is to obtain data from where it currently resides, changing it to be compatible in format with the desired destination and putting it into the destination system. These three steps are called extract, transform, and load (ETL). All data integration, regardless of whether it is performed in batch or real time, synchronously or asynchronously, physically or virtually, revolves around these basic actions. Although it is an extremely simple concept, large possible differences in designs and technology solutions exist for implementation. There are development and support roles with titles that begin with ETL (and other related acronyms) for the analysts, modelers, and programmers who develop these functions.

Many vendor packages exist for performing ETL, some of which are specialized for particular styles of data integration in varying levels of complexity and prices. Some of the available packages are extremely complicated, and most require programmers with specialized training and experience in the particular package or tool in order to effectively implement solutions.

Profiling

Profiling data involves reviewing and analyzing the actual data potentially to be included in an extract to further understand the format and content. Profiling should be performed when potential data for an extract has been identified through high-level requirements gathering.

It can sometimes be difficult to arrange for profiling because getting access authority for the person who is to perform the profiling, or the results analyst, may involve sensitive or personal information. It is critical to the success of the project that profiling not be skipped and that acceptable access authority be granted to enable this step to be performed. Profiling has been found to be absolutely essential to developing extracts that meet business needs. Profiling is used to confirm that the format and content of the source data meet the description given from business users, metadata, and documentation. In cases where one or more of these levels of documentation do not exist, profiling can be used to develop the necessary metadata and documentation. In practice, profiling usually identifies substantial differences from what was expected in the actual source data and can help to prevent unexpected project delays.

Profiling tools can be used to report the inferred format and content from the actual source data: percentage of null or blank contents, number of distinct values and instances with highest occurrences, and format of contents. Some profiling tools can even find relationships between data across data stores, using the field names or the actual field contents to infer relationships.

During data profiling, it is often found that the source data may need to be corrected and cleaned prior to implementation of ETL. In some cases the corrections can be automated, but it is more frequently the case that the corrections have to be done manually by a businessperson familiar with the data. A business decision must be made as to whether the corrections are made in the source data structure or whether the problems found with the data will be passed on to the target data store.

No one wants to hear about unexpected issues found with the source data. Issues involving the source data can greatly affect project time estimates and resource requirements. However, the earlier in the project life cycle that issues are uncovered, the smaller the impact will be. It is critically important that profiling is performed early in the project life cycle to minimize the impact to the projects that are planning to use the data.

Extract

In order to perform the "extract" part of ETL, it is necessary to access the data in the system or data store in which it currently resides. A basic understanding of the format and meaning of the data is needed to select what data of interest is to be copied.

There are two basic approaches to extracting data: Either the current system, the source system, makes a copy of the data, or another system, say a specialized extract system, comes in and grabs the data. The benefit of the source system taking the extract is that the system currently storing the data (and the current system support staff) understands the meaning of the data and, of course, the technological solution in which it is stored. However, multiple potential resource problems arise when the source system performs the extract. Frequently, the source systems from which we want to extract data are production operational systems and we don't want to negatively impact their production performance by adding more operations than they were designed to perform. Also, the source system support staff may be too busy to create an extract, may not be trained in the technology or tools being used for the extract, or may not consider the extract to be a priority.

Using a specialized extract application to pull data from the system currently storing the data has the smallest impact on the source system, although there is probably still some use of the data store engine, such as the database management system or the file management system, and so there may still be some resource contention. A specialized extract application would be staffed with personnel trained in using the specific extract tools and technology.

In practice, however, it frequently works best if the source system support staff creates the extract. Knowledge of the system and technology in which the data currently resides, as well as the format and meaning of the source data, tends to be the biggest stumbling block in trying to centralize extract development. Most specialized extract applications are efficient at extracting data from relational databases, either with generic SQL adapters or with specialized adapters for the particular database management system (DBMS). Many of these tools struggle with the oddities inherent in mainframe file structures, such as a COBOL REDEFINES (COmmon Business-Oriented Language structure in which various data attributes may be present) and other specific data storage technology structures.

Staging

The extract process implies that the result of the extract will be a "file" of data that will then be copied and transported to another location, usually another server or platform. Storing the extracted file on the source server platform and storing the extracted data copied onto the target server platform, as well as any intermediate points, is called "staging the data". There is commonly a staging point on the source system server platform as well the target. Staging the data allows for an audit trail of what was sent and what was received. It also allows timing the processing of the data between the source and target systems to be loosely coupled, or asynchronous: The two systems do not have to be coordinated to process the data at the same time, but they can do so when it is most appropriate for each separately, as long as the extract from the source system occurs first.

However, reading and writing from disk, called I/O (for input/output), is significantly slower than processing in memory. Bypassing staging points in the design of an ETL solution may make the process as much as ten times faster, a significant difference when speed is critical, but would lose the benefits of the audit trail and loose system coupling.

Access layers

In order to design an extract solution, it is usually necessary to understand the various security access layers involved in protecting the data to be extracted, although some or all of the layers may be logically hidden or virtualized, where managing the access is performed automatically. The access layers involved include at least the organization network and firewall layers, the server layer (or physical layer), the operating system layer, the application layer, and the data structure layer.

Where integration is across organizations, there is a security access layer that may have to be crossed into an organization's area of concern. Frequently, this is logically implemented with firewalls protecting networks. We constantly access data on the Internet virtually using Internet protocols, where a logical address is located within a particular organization on a particular server. Most organizations separate their internal activity from their interactions with external organizations and systems by implementing separate networks for each separated by firewalls (logical protection) and very carefully designed limited abilities to move data between the two. The logical area where interactions are made with external systems is referred to as the "DMZ" or demilitarized zone—a reference to demarcation areas between combatant forces during war.

Different systems and data stores are frequently located on different physical servers, although the separation of servers may not be physical but may be using logical partitioning and cloud computing technologies. Access to the server (logical or physical) will have its own security protection. Physical and logical servers will run operating system software that will also contain access security capabilities.

If an extract process is accessing data using the application code API (application programming interface), a best practice, then the extract process may have to pass through the application security access layer. Ultimately, the data structure storing the data to be extracted, whether it is a database management system or a file storage system, will also have a security access layer.

Some of these access layers will be irrelevant, if an extract process is running in the same organization's network as the source and target, or if the extract process bypasses the application layer to access the data structure directly. Most of the access will be through logical layers that manage the complexity automatically with registries, such as a private cloud or database management system, where the physical server location of the data is virtualized by the access layer and need not be known by the extract process. However, in designing an extract process, it will be necessary to know how all the security access layers are or are not being implemented.

Data security is also frequently implemented using data masking, which limits or encrypts data of particular sensitivity or confidentiality while allowing access to the rest of the data in the data structure. This method is useful for allowing technologists, programmers, or consultants to analyze data in a data structure while limiting access to particularly sensitive information. Data masking may be implemented by transforming the data in question or by limiting access through the query.

Transform

The process of transforming data to be compatible with the target data structure may vary from being extremely simple to being impossible, or may require the collection of additional information. The transformation process requires detailed business requirements that the business owners of the data in question have either developed or approved, whereas the extract and load processes may be almost wholly technical processes requiring very little business review except to ensure that the correct data is being extracted.

Simple mapping

The simplest type of transformation is that in which an individual text or numeric field is defined and formatted consistently in both the source and target and simply has to be "mapped" between the two: It is specified that the particular source field should be copied to the particular target field. It might be almost as simple to make a slight adjustment in format, either because of differing technical implementations in the source and target or slight definition differences such as the target being somewhat larger than the source field.

Lookups

A field in a data source may contain only one of a set of possible values that must be transformed to one of a different set in the target. The requirements will have to specify the mappings from source values to target values. If the source field is text and the target field is a set of possible values, then the transformation may have to be performed through a combination of string manipulation and manual data standardization.

Aggregation and normalization

Frequently, the transformation of data is much more complex than these simple cases suggest. Determining the value in the target data structure may require retrieving multiple pieces of data from the source that may be in various structures. One record or row of data in the source may map to multiple records in the target, or vice versa.

Where there are multiple sources of the same data there may have to be rules specified that indicate how to determine if two pieces of source data represent the same entity in the target and how to determine which source should be used if the information is different in the multiple sources. This type of processing is called "matching" and is a sophisticated area used especially in master data management (MDM).

Calculation

The values to be stored in the target data structures may have to be derived from other data using some type of formula based on business rules or data quality rules in cases where the source is missing or lacking.

Ultimately, the data in the source data structure may be insufficient to provide the data required in the target data structure. The business requirements in this case may specify defaulting the target values, or a separate effort may be required to collect the required data through another internal or external source or manual operation.

It is important that profiling of the source and, if possible, the target data has occurred prior to finalizing the transformation requirements, since it is normal to find formats and contents during profiling that were not expected or previously documented. As with profiling, no one wants to hear about problems specifying data transformation, and it is critical that transformation business requirements are created early in any project so that additional required data collection can be planned and performed in a timely fashion. Business requirements for transformation must be reviewed and approved by businesspeople familiar with the data in question, as technical analysts and programmers may miss business implications and should not have final responsibility for these decisions.

Load

The "load" part of ETL has to do with getting the data into the target data structure. There is some discussion of whether the most efficient order of processing is extract, transform, load or rather extract, load, transform, the difference having to do with whether the transformation step should occur on the source server or the target server (or a separate server). This discussion is very relevant with regard to high-volume processing and to which engine will be able to do so fastest. Whether there are staging points for the extracted data at one or more points in the process will greatly affect the speed of processing as well. Ultimately, the last step in the ETL is getting the data into the target data structure, either physical or virtual.

The two main approaches to loading data into the target data store are either to write code to insert the data directly or to utilize the application code that already exists for inserting data into the target data store. Whenever possible, it is greatly preferable to use the existing application code, since built into this code is an understanding of how the data is supposed to be structured in the target data store. It is possible that the current application code is not written for high- volume loads and cannot be used in the load window available. Still, tuning the load process to enable use of the current application code is preferable to writing independent code to use for data load.

When the target data store is part of a purchased package, there are two additional reasons for using the application code to load data. Many purchased packages specify that all data must be loaded through their code because the data structures by themselves do not sufficiently describe the format of the data expected by the application. Package vendors usually provide an API code that is recommended to be used to insert data into the target data store. Custom or legacy applications may not have formal API code available for use, but it is best to try to reuse the code that normally inserts the data into the data stores in order to load the data. This code may not be accessible. or it may be insufficient for reasons such as defaulting dates to current date.

Regardless of which method of loading data is used, data validation rules built into the target data structures should not be disabled during the load process unless it is absolutely certain that all validation checks are being done prior to the data load process. Frequently, technicians will suggest that the loads can be done more swiftly with the data rules turned off, but there was a reason these were defined in the first place, and data that does not follow those encoded data business rules are not meant to be in the target data structure. A process must be in place for reporting and resolving errors with the data to be loaded.

Data Warehousing

INFORMATION IN THIS CHAPTER

What is data warehousing?

Data warehouses are data constructs (and associated applications) used as central repositories of data to provide consistent sources for analysis and reporting. Enterprise data warehouses (EDWs) are created for the entire organization to be able to analyze information from across the entire organization. Frequently, very large organizations will have multiple enterprise data warehouses, each having data either from large parts of the organization, such as regions, or from large functional areas. Batch data integration solutions are generally used for putting data into and taking data out of a data warehouse. Data warehousing architectures are designed to have consistent data available for the entire organization to use for analysis, to format data particularly for analysis and reporting purposes, to take the stress of analytical reporting needs off the operational systems, and to allow for historical snapshots data.[1]

Data integration techniques are so critical to the functioning data warehouse that some experts in data warehousing consider data integration to be a subset of data warehousing architecture techniques. However, data integration is critical to other data management areas as well and is an independent area of data management practice.

Layers in an enterprise data warehouse architecture

Data coming into the data warehouse and leaving the data warehouse use extract, transform, and load (ETL) to pass through logical structural layers of the architecture that are connected using data integration technologies, as depicted in Figure 7.1, where the data passes from left to right, from source systems to the data warehouse and then to the business intelligence layer. In many organizations, the enterprise data warehouse is the primary user of data integration and may have sophisticated vendor data integration tools specifically to support the data warehousing requirements. Data integration provides the flow of data between the various layers of the data warehouse architecture, entering and leaving.

Operational application layer

The operational application layer consists of the various sources of data to be fed into the data warehouse from the applications that perform the primary operational functions of the organization. This layer is where the portfolio of core application systems for the organization resides. Not all reporting is necessarily transferred to the data warehouse. Operational reporting concerning the processing within a particular application may remain within the application because the concerns are specific to the particular functionality and needs associated with the users of the application.

External data

Some data for the data warehouse may be coming from outside the organization. Data may be supplied for the warehouse, with further detail sourced from the organization's customers, suppliers, or other partners. Standard codes, valid values, and other reference data may be provided from government sources, industry organizations, or business exchanges. Additionally, many data warehouses enhance the data available in the organization with purchased data concerning consumers or customers.

---

[1]Inmon, W. H. *Building the Data Warehouse* (Hoboken, NJ: John Wiley & Sons, 1992).

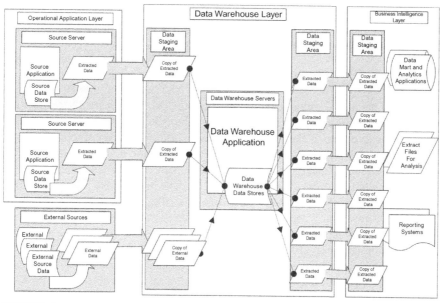

FIGURE 7.1

Data Warehouse Data Flow.

External data must pass through additional security access layers for the network and organization, protecting the organization from harmful data and attacks.

External data should be viewed as less likely to conform to the expected structure of its contents, since communication and agreement between separate organizations is usually somewhat harder than communications within the same organization. Profiling and quality monitoring of data acquired from external sources is very important, even more critical, possibly, than for monitoring data from internal sources. Integration with external data should be kept loosely coupled with the expectation of potential changes in format and content.

Data staging areas coming into a data warehouse

Data coming into a data warehouse is usually staged, or stored in the original source format, in order to allow a loose coupling of the timing between the source and the data warehouse in terms of when the data is sent from the source and when it is loaded into the warehouse. The data staging area also allows for an audit trail of what data was sent, which can be used to analyze problems with data found in the warehouse or in reports.

There is usually a staging area located with each of the data sources, as well as a staging area for all data coming in to the warehouse.

Some data warehouse architectures include an operational data store (ODS) for having data available real time or near real time for analysis and reporting. Real-time data integration techniques will be described in later sections of this book.

Data warehouse data structure

The data in the data warehouse is usually formatted into a consistent logical structure for the enterprise, no longer dependent on the structure of the various sources of data. The structure of data in the data warehouse may be optimized for quick loading of high volumes of data from the various sources. If some analysis is performed directly on data in the warehouse, it may also be structured for efficient high-volume access, but usually that is done in separate data marts and specialized analytical structures in the business intelligence layer.

Metadata concerning data in the data warehouse is very important for its effective use and is an important part of the data warehouse architecture: a clear understanding of the meaning of the data (business metadata), where it came from or its lineage (technical metadata), and when things happened (operational metadata). The metadata associated with the data in the warehouse should accompany the data that is provided to the business intelligence layer for analysis.

Staging from data warehouse to data mart or business intelligence

There may be separate staging areas for data coming out of the data warehouse and into the business intelligence structures in order to provide loose coupling and audit trails, as described earlier for data coming into the data warehouse. However, since writing data to disk and reading from disk (I/O operations) are very slow compared with processing, it may be deemed more efficient to tightly couple the data warehouse and business intelligence structures and skip much of the overhead of staging data coming out of the data warehouse as well as going into the business intelligence structures. An audit trail between the data warehouse and data marts may be a low priority, as it is less important than when the data was last acquired or updated in the data warehouse and in the source application systems. Speed in making the data available for analysis is a larger concern.

Business Intelligence Layer

The business intelligence layer focuses on storing data efficiently for access and analysis.

Data marts are data structures created for providing to a particular part of an organization data relevant to their analytical needs, structured for fast access. Data marts may also be for enterprise-wide use but using specialized structures or technologies.

Extract files from the data warehouse are requested for local user use, for analysis, and for preparation of reports and presentations. Extract files should not usually be manually loaded into analytical and reporting systems. Besides the inefficiency of manually transporting data between systems, the data may be changed in the process between the data warehouse and the target system, losing the chain of custody information that would concern an auditor. A more effective and trusted audit trail is created by automatically feeding data between systems.

Extract files are sometimes also needed to be passed to external organizations and entities. As with all data passing out from the data warehouse, metadata fully describing the data should accompany extract files leaving the organization.

Data from the data warehouse may also be fed into highly specialized reporting systems, such as for customer statement or regulatory reporting, which may have their own data structures or may read data directly from the data warehouse.

Data in the business intelligence layer may be accessed using internal or external web solutions, specialized reporting and analytical tools, or generic desktop tools. Appropriate access authority and audit trails should be stored tracking all data accesses into the data warehouse or business intelligence layers.

Types of data to load in a data warehouse

The various types of data to be loaded into the data warehouse are treated differently and have different life cycles. Some data is kept synchronized with data in the transaction system and only changes are tracked and passed into the data warehouse, while for other types of data a "snapshot" is taken at regular periods of the full set of data regardless of whether there has been any changes and the data is fully replicated each time data is loaded into the data warehouse.

Master data in a data warehouse

Master data is the data about the important items in an organization by which one would want to sort information such as customers, products, suppliers, and employees. Reference data is the set of valid values associated with certain fields and may overlap somewhat with master data in that one may want to view data sorted by reference data and it may be dynamic and have to be updated frequently: geographic areas, organizational hierarchies, industry codes. Both master data and reference data may include hierarchical information or associations between items such as companies being owned by other companies or states located within countries. The full expression of hierarchical information with explicit data instances, such as the specific zip codes within each state and the states in a country, is known as a taxonomy.

In data warehousing, master data and reference data are extremely important because these are the items by which people want to sort and display information and around which data is being consolidated for the enterprise (or the scope of the data warehouse). When structuring the data in the data warehouse and in the business intelligence layer, the items by which the data is usually sorted are called the dimensions. Therefore, in data warehousing and business intelligence the terms *master data* and *dimensions* are frequently used as synonyms.

Usually, the primary sources of the master data and reference data are outside the data warehouse and any changes, additions, or deletions to the master data are fed into the data warehouse before associated transactions are loaded. Changes to master data and reference data may be fed to the data warehouse as soon they occur in the source system or on a periodic basis such as daily, weekly, or monthly, as long as it is the same or more frequently than the transaction data associated.

In the data warehouse, changes to master data and reference data will be stored with associated effective start and end dates indicating when the changes are valid. Usually data in the data warehouse is structured to enable fast high-volume loading rather than fast high-volume retrieval. If structuring the data for query, however, the master data changes may be structured in three alternate ways: as if the master data was always in its current effective state; as if the changes to the master data created a new piece of master data; or the change to the master data with its start and end effective dates associated. An example is if a customer reaches an elite classification level. Should queries on that customer show all their history in the elite classification or only the transactions following the point at which the customer became elite? The data can be structured for query either way or is able to do both, but it can be confusing to leave the decision open to the query; different analysis may report different results, depending on slight differences in making the query.

In the staging area coming into the data warehouse, it is usually necessary to have a cross-reference table (or tables) to translate the identifiers and codes assigned to the master data and reference data in the various operational applications to those used in the data warehouse. These cross references themselves may have updates that are automatically fed from a source, possibly the master data applications, or updates may be a manual data warehouse system support activity that must be coordinated with any changes to codes used in the source applications.

Master or reference data that is used as a primary item for sorting and searching in the data warehouse or in data marts is called a "dimension".[2] Depending on the velocity of change of a particular set of master data or reference data, it may be described as a slowly changing or rapidly changing dimension. Rapidly changing dimensions may have to be specially tuned to handle particularly high volumes or high rates of change.

Balance and snapshot data in a data warehouse

Usually, the information on any kind of balance information from source applications, such as an inventory balance or currency balance, is copied as a point-in-time snapshot on a periodic basis, such as daily, weekly, or monthly, but might

---

[2]Kimball, R. The Data Warehouse Toolkit (New York, John Wiley & Sons, 2002).

be smaller increments such as hourly. So, a copy of the entire set of balances is sent from the operational applications to the data warehouse. Any master data associated with the balances is transformed using the cross-reference tables in staging, and the balances are stored in the data warehouse with the appropriate point-in-time interval, the date, or the time the balance was copied.

With multiple snapshots of a balance, historical analysis on the data can be made across the balances associated with a particular piece of master data (or dimension).

Transactional data in a data warehouse

There are two types of transactions: business transactions that have a life cycle with multiple events and statuses, and accounting transactions that post as credits and debits and offsets but are never changed. Each transaction is usually associated with each of the dimensions in the data warehouse such as customer, product, geography, organizational structure, or standard industry codes.

Accounting types of transactions are only added to the data warehouse, never changed. New accounting transactions since the last time an extract was taken from the operational applications are copied and passed to the data warehouse, or when a new accounting transaction is added to the operational application a copy is passed to the data warehouse.

Business transactions can be managed in multiple ways with a data warehouse. Either periodic snapshots are taken of the business transactions or updates to the business transactions are passed to the data warehouse. Usually within the data warehouse only one copy of the business transaction is kept with the history of when events surrounding the transaction occurred and when the status of the transaction changed. Keeping multiple snapshots of a business transaction in the data warehouse is rare, as analysis is usually on the events that caused changes or across transactions rather than on the state of a particular transaction over time.

Business transactions, depending on the type of business, may each have very long life cycles. Sometimes business transactions themselves are treated as master data or dimensions, such as a contract or account.

Events

Events are things that occur at a point in time. They may be business transactions or be associated with business transactions. They are usually associated with the dimensions in the data warehouse. Events are like accounting transactions in their behavior: They are added to the data warehouse but usually are not updated.

Reconciliation

Periodic checks should be made that the data sent from the operational application systems and other sources into the data warehouse were received and saved correctly. Comparison of number of items sent and received as well as a comparison of financial totals should be made for each source and type of data. Within the data warehouse periodic checks should be made that events and transactions add up to balance changes.

A SIDEBAR FROM THE AUTHOR . . . ON DATA WAREHOUSING AND PROFILING

In my own experience, profiling is critical to data warehousing projects, as well as to every data-oriented project. Most data warehouse projects that I have worked on or observed have had an unexpected period just prior to going live where parts of the data structures have to be redesigned and other significant changes made because the data in the data warehouse does not match what was expected, because the data in the source systems was different than assumed, described, or documented in existing metadata.

In one data warehouse project where I was acting as the data modeler and managing the DBAs (database administrators), a senior business analyst approached me with some independent (and unscheduled) analysis he had performed: The data coming from the accounting system looked entirely different from what we had been expecting in both content of each individual record and the number of records. We were unprepared for the large volume of records being generated from the accounting system, where we were interested in only a small number of the types of records. Also, the content of individual records was extremely different than expected, and multiple records from the accounting system would be needed to acquire the full set of information we were expecting from each record. This discovery required me to redesign a section of the data warehouse logical model and add a new processing section to the data warehouse functionality to compute the information we were expecting from groups of accounting transactions. Luckily, we made this discovery early in the code development stage of the project, and so we were able to make the corrections to the model and requirements and add the extra coding requirements without affecting the overall project.

From this and other similar experiences, I learned that data profiling of production data is a required analysis activity that cannot be skipped from the life cycle of any data-oriented project and should be performed before requirements are completed. Tension frequently exists between the need to perform profiling as part of analysis and the need to keep production data private, but in choosing battles to fight in a data warehouse project, this is not the battle to skip and usually an acceptable compromise can be reached or months should be added to the implementation schedule for redesign needed prior to system implementation.

INTERVIEW WITH AN EXPERT: KRISH KRISHNAN ON DATA WAREHOUSING AND DATA INTEGRATION

Following is an interview with Krish Krishnan on the importance and use of data integration in data warehousing.

Krish Krishnan has spent 12 years designing, architecting and developing data warehouse solutions, in the last five years focusing on unstructured data integration into the data warehouse. He has been involved in some of the largest and most complex designs and architecture of next-generation data warehouses. He is co-author of "*Building the Unstructured Data Warehouse*" with Bill Inmon.

How is data integration (i.e., moving and transforming data) related to data warehousing?

The underlying goal of data warehousing is to create an enterprise platform for providing a unified view of data in a single, integrated environment. The data in this environment is cleansed, transformed, and ready for consumption by the downstream applications. Data integration is the layer of processing data that manages all these activities, including movement, quality management, and transformation of data.

The most complex activity in data integration is the transformation from one format to another, which includes cleaning, standardization, enrichment, and metadata processing.

The absence of a data integration layer for the data warehouse would certainly lead to colossal failures as data within the data warehouse would be loosely integrated, repetitive, and possibly processed multiple times for each business rule. The end state of such a chaotic architecture is the failure of the data warehouse. Hence, data integration is an integral part of the data warehouse for both structured and unstructured data.

How and why is data moved for data warehousing?

Data is the heartbeat of a data warehouse. In order for information to be current in a data warehouse, there is a continuum of data movement from different types of source applications to the data warehouse. In a traditional setup, the processing of data is divided into collection, transportation, cleansing, enrichment, and integration. There are multiple techniques to move and process data including

- ETL—The most common approach is extract, transform, and load," known as ETL. Source data is collected from different data generators and processed to an intermediate layer called the staging area (optionally to an operational data store on some designs). The data is cleansed and enriched in the staging environment, which is the first transformation exercise, and further processed into the data warehouse, where the business rules and data integration rules are applied as the larger transformation.
- ELT—Another popular approach is called extract, load, and transform (ELT). In this approach, the data is extracted from the source applications and databases, loaded into the staging area with data enrichment and cleansing rules applied, and further processed into the data warehouse for pure integration-related transformation. This approach is preferred in situations where data is agile and very structured in nature, and requires minimal integration.
- CDC—A third technique is called change data capture (CDC), where a third-party application is installed on the source systems to collect changes occurring to the data. This method normally retrieves changes from the database log, an efficient approach that doesn't impact the source database. The changes are then extracted from the source and moved to the data warehouse. On the target side, the same third-party application is installed to process the data collected from every extract and load it into the data warehouse staging area. The data is then cleansed, enriched, and transformed to its final destination within the data warehouse. CDC is very useful for processing data in a near real-time situation where the data availability is very critical. In certain architectures, the CDC data is directly loaded into the ODS for operational purposes and then loaded to the data warehouse staging layers.

There are many custom derivations of the three techniques, and often a hybrid approach is adopted to satisfy the multiple competing requirements from the data warehouse for current data.

What kinds of transformations are done to the data being moved to the data warehousing? (e.g., different data structures, conforming data structures, dimensional models)

Several data transformations can be done with data processing to a data warehouse. The baseline transformation is to extract data from the source systems and move it into an integrated model in the data warehouse, which means a transformation from a highly normalized structure to a transformed and denormalized or dimensional structure. The transformations include the following.

- Data denormalization—transform highly normalized structures to a denormalized data warehouse format. Popular with the top-down or Inmon approach to building a data warehouse.
- Dimensionalization—transform high normalized structure into dimensions and facts; a bottom-up approach or Kimball star schema model of a data warehouse.
- Metadata processing—integrate a business vocabulary with the data as it is processed in the data warehouse. Enables harmonization of different nomenclatures into one single definition.
- Master Data processing—transform key structures of data to conform to a master data set, creating a highly integrated layer of data.
- Generating surrogate keys—using a common technique for dimensional data transformation to preserve history, create surrogate keys in the data warehouse.
- Coding data—create lookup tables and lists for compressing duplicate data
- Pivoting data—employ multidimensional data transformation for loading data
- Splitting data—change multivalued columns to single columns
- Merging data—integrate data into single tables or data structures
- Lookup data—create and enrich lookup data. Lookup data is a reference library where the identity value for the data is substituted in the place of the actual data.

Apart from the data transformations mentioned in this section, there are data model and data architecture-driven transformations through which the data undergoes several layers of transformations. Then the aggregate and hierarchy drill down transformations and semantic layer transformations form the next set of transformations for data to be consumed by the business users.

An often-overlooked transformation is the physical database-driven transformation where tables are split vertically, partitioned into discrete structures, indexed, and sorted for better optimization at storage.

These multiple transformations are the major operations in moving data to the data warehouse.

Are there different data Integration considerations for putting data into a data warehouse different than from taking data out of a data warehouse?

Absolutely, yes, the data integration considerations for moving data into the data warehouse are to integrate the data for consumption by the business and other users. The inbound transformations will be to migrate the data from OLTP-like structures to a data warehouse model, which is mostly dimensional in nature or, at least, is more denormalized than the on-line transaction processing (OLTP) structures.

On the other hand, extracting data from the data warehouse for downstream applications will be to satisfy specific reporting or analytical requirements. The data extracted for these purposes will be different in layout and structure. Typically, the data extracted for these purposes will include the transformed data structure and all the reference data, copies of master data, metadata, and any special data such as geospatial. In the extraction process of the data from the data warehouse, the data is extracted to maintain the referential integrity as it was loaded to the data warehouse; this is different from the referential integrity model of the base OLTP applications.

How is data warehousing for structured data different from data warehousing for unstructured data? Is the data integration different?

Data warehousing for structured data has a defined cycle. We start with requirements, then move to data modeling. Once we create the data model, we acquire and transform data to be stored into this data model for integration and downstream processing. This is a very read-efficient operation inasmuch as we can define the final state structure and once data is loaded, the reads from the structures are very efficient.

Data warehousing for unstructured data is very volatile in nature. We cannot anticipate the type of data, its format, structure, and quality of information until the data is acquired. The data model for this data is created after processing the data. This type of data processing is called "schema-less." The data is ingested as files and processed as files.

In processing unstructured data, all the acquisition and processing of data is done prior to finding the data elements that can be used for integration with the data warehouse. In this approach there is no data integration, in a traditional sense, yet there is data integration from an analytics perspective.

Have you seen any data warehousing projects where data integration issues led to significant problems?

Yes, in my experience as an architect and an expert consultant, I have personally seen programs fail when clients have not understood the need to build a robust data integration architecture. In many situations where architects and managers of data warehouses have called for an independent expert opinion on the reasons for failure, evaluations of the underlying problems have pointed to poor data integration architecture.

The most common impact that I have seen from poor data integration in a data warehouse include

- Data quality problems
- Multiple values for a single column
- Date and time format problems
- Character sets and language translation
- Unicode support issues
- Currency formats

Poor data integration architecture has brought some of the best designed data warehouses to its knees and caused deployment failure and cost overruns.

Have you had experiences where particular attention was paid to data integration in data warehousing?

Yes. There are some brilliant data integration architectures that have created a success story for these data warehouses. The processing complexity of these warehouses is of the highest order: They run in a 24 $\times$ 7 service mode and have very stringent performance requirements. With such tight deadlines, the only failproof method to process data is by designing a scalable and flexible data integration architecture.

The impressive aspect of this architecture is its ability to process multinational and multilingual data sets into a global data warehouse, with data enrichment, transformation, transportation, and integration all rolled into the processing architecture. Some of these clients have been awarded best practices awards for their adherence to a very efficient data integration design.

Have you had experiences where data integration was neglected on a data warehousing project?

In most of the projects that I have worked on as an architect or a consultant, the emphasis has been on the aspect of data integration. In some situations the client decided against implementing a full data integration architecture, and the team had to face several hurdles to implement the data warehouse. As end results of these situations, the cycle time to implement was twice or three times the original duration and the cost was three times the original cost for development.

Do you think there should be a separate staging area for loading data into a data warehouse? Why or why not?

I definitely support the need for a staging area for the data warehouse. The primary reason for this architectural decision arises from the fact that we need to acquire and preprocess data and perform data-cleansing activities before loading the data to the data warehouse. Whether you decide to have an active or real-time data warehouse or the traditional Kimball architecture of conformed dimensions, without a separate area for the complex data integration activities the real scalability and flexibility of the data warehouse cannot be complete. In most of the programs in which I have participated, I have always built and deployed a staging area.

Are there special considerations relating to the movement of metadata in a data warehouse, i.e., how is the business, operational, and technical metadata of data in the data warehouse passed to the business intelligence layer or accessed from the business intelligence layer?

Metadata has been the most ignored aspect of 90 percent of the world's data warehouses. In many cases, there are multiple teams from business analysis to design, development, and deployment of the data warehouse, and each one often blames the other for not maintaining metadata.

In my opinion, metadata of different types needs to be developed in the data warehouse. The business metadata is defined during the requirements phase, and this metadata is implemented in the semantic layers and database views. Technical metadata is implemented in the data processing, data model, and physical database design and business intelligence layers. For the business intelligence layer, most of the software packages today provide a metadata integration layer.

Metadata has to be migrated across the layers of the data warehouse along with the data itself. Without this architectural implementation, the data warehouse will fail. In fact, to implement an integration of unstructured data, the metadata layer is the key.

Web 2.0-based data architectures rely heavily on metadata layers for data integration and processing across multiple databases.

Do you think people neglect data integration in data warehousing? If so, why?

In many cases data warehouse architects, designers, and managers consider the data integration architecture and implementation to be expensive, and so they usually cut corners in this development activity, only to end up spending two or more times the amount to complete the development of the data warehouse. Also, people often assume that data processing software will automatically address data integration and overlook the planning for this important activity.

What kinds of tools or technologies are used to support data integration for data warehousing?

In a typical structured data processing architecture, ETL, ELT, CDC, service oriented architecture (SOA), and Custom-coded software packages are implemented for data movement; data quality tools are implemented for data cleansing; master data management tools are implemented for reference data processing; and metadata reference libraries are implemented for managing metadata.

Are the tools for data integration for data warehousing different for structured and unstructured data?

Yes, for unstructured data integration the tools used include Hadoop, NoSQL databases, and textual ETL engines. Some traditional data integration vendors have announced support for unstructured data integration, but these are still in primitive stages of evolution. The special technologies can process unstructured data of multiple formats in large volumes.

How do you think the area of data warehousing is changing? In what direction do you think this area is headed?

Data warehousing as a concept is here to stay for a longer period of time. However, the rapid change occurring in the space is the integration of unstructured data into the data warehouse and the momentum to incorporate Hadoop as the corporate data repository while retaining the enterprise data warehouse to process complex analytics. The future of data warehouse is going to evolve as a semantic interface-driven data repository based on the relational databases and unstructured technology architectures that will provide answers to all sorts of queries from enterprise users.

Do you think the technologies for performing data warehousing, especially around data integration, are changing?

Definitely, yes, the data integration technologies are changing to support unstructured data integration. This requires a significant engineering effort from the provider community. Another popular technique is to use data visualization tools to create a data discovery environment for pre-processing and analysis of unstructured data.

Data Conversion

8

INFORMATION IN THIS CHAPTER

What is data conversion?

When implementing a new application system or changing operations from one application system to another, it is necessary to populate the data structures of the new application system. Sometimes the data structures of the new application system are empty, and other times, when consolidating applications, there is already data in the new data structure and it is necessary to add to it. All the same techniques and strategies are necessary as described in the section on extract, transform, and load, as well as much from the section on Data Warehousing.

Data conversion life cycle

The basic systems development life cycle for a data conversion project is the same as for any application development endeavor, with activity centered around planning, analysis, requirements, development, testing, and implementation. A pure "waterfall" methodology is not implied or necessary. Like other data-related projects, the activities in the analysis phase should include profiling the data in the source and target data structures. The requirements phase should include verifying that the assumptions made are true by trying the load of very small amounts of data. Unlike application development projects, there is no support phase in the data conversion life cycle, unless additional data sources are to be loaded to the target application later, such as when multiple systems are being consolidated over time, data is being moved from one system to another in phases, or an organizational merger or acquisition takes place.

Data conversion analysis

Analysis and planning for data conversion should be started as early as possible, as soon as analysis and planning for using the new application are completed. Too frequently, data conversion is thought of as a quick, last-minute activity, and this view may then cause delay to the entire application implementation and problems with the converted data. In some cases, this may necessitate falling back to the original application and create serious customer service issues. In truth, a new application implementation should begin with data conversion planning. If the data conversion activities can get started early enough, then the data conversion development process can provide the data for all stages of testing, not just the final phase of user testing, which must include converted data.

An assessment should include identifying which data areas need to be converted. This basic decision should be performed and approved by business and technology subject matter experts from both the source and target systems before a detailed estimate of the data conversion effort can be performed. This would include a list of significant reference data, a specific list of master data, as well as transactions, events, and balance data areas. Then some profiling of the source data should be performed to determine the volume and quality of the source data. Sometimes this initial assessment of the source data shows that the data may be of insufficient quality in some way for the target application system. It therefore becomes necessary to add another track to clean or enhance the source data prior to conversion. Of course it is much better to make this determination as early in the data conversion project as possible.

Best practice data loading

Whenever available, data conversion should use the target application API to load data into the target data structures. This is best practice for data conversion and for any data loading that doesn't use the application data entry front end. Many vendor package applications insist that all data loading should be through the provided API. Should an API be unavailable or insufficient for data conversion needs, an assessment should be made as to whether it is more cost effective and less risky for some of the data, say the master data and reference data, be added to the application manually. It should be kept in mind that data conversion is not performed just once but needs to be repeated many, many times throughout the testing process. Thus, data that is manually added needs to be backed up and restored at the beginning of each data conversion and application test cycle.

If a sufficient application API is not available, then it may be necessary to load data directly into the data structure of the new application, the target data structure.

Improving source data quality

Issues associated with data quality tend to become highlighted when using the data for something different than its original or previous use. Therefore, when loading data into a data warehouse for the first time or converting to a new application data structure, problems with the data may be uncovered.

During the analysis phase of a data conversion project, it is best practice to profile the data in the source data structures and assess whether the quality of the data is sufficient for use in the new application. This is not a search for perfection in the data quality but only seeks to identify whether a special project needs to be performed to improve the data prior to production conversion. Issues with the data may include data that does not meet the business rules requirements of the target application or data that is missing required information. The source system may not have a place to store data required for the target application, or the field in the source system is not currently or fully populated. Most frequently, the data requiring cleansing or enhancing is master data.

It may sometimes be possible to perform enhancement or data improvement projects automatically through custom code or by acquiring the missing data and enhancing the source data automatically. Usually, the data is improved manually by the source operations business team or by temporary business staff who research and enhance the source data to bring it up to the standard required for conversion to the target application.

Mapping to target

Whether loading data using an API or directly into the application data structure, an important recommendation is to focus on the target data layout and then determine where that data may be obtained. Possibly because the staff working on a data conversion project need to be most knowledgeable of the source system—and so they tend to focus on what they know best—in practice the data conversion staff spend too much time focusing on the source data structures and not enough time on the target data layout and structure.

In developing the mapping requirements for mapping data from source to target, best practice is to start with the target data layout and then find where in the source the data can be found. Before starting development using these requirements, one should test manually, entering data through the front end, and verify that the data is loaded by the application into the positions in the target data structure that was anticipated. It is also a good idea to test that an API works as anticipated, before entering the development stage. Because the behavior of the target application from the names of data fields or metadata can be very risky, assumptions should be verified by testing.

A double check should be performed at the end of the requirements process that important aspects of the source data are not being ignored. Items that are possibly being left behind in the data conversion should be highlighted and approved. Sometimes important functionality in the source system that is not in the target system should be brought to light.

The target data structures may be modeled or configured and the source structures may be considered as the model for the target. Using the physical data structures of an application being retired is tricky, since the application system may have existing limitations inherent in the data structures or related to the particular technology implementation. If a modeling activity for the target data structures is needed, that activity should be as independent of the source data structures as possible and the source data model should only be used as a double check that all required data has been accounted for in the target model.

Configuration data

In a new implementation of a purchased vendor application, there are usually configuration settings for the application that are stored in the application data structures: business rules, field definitions, and edits, as well as a vast set of other data that must be set up appropriately in order for the target application to run as expected. This information should be classified as reference data or may have its own category of configuration data. This configuration information should be treated as application code that has to go through change control and application testing before being changed in a production environment. Frequently, the proper settings for this data are obtained from the target application implementation team, and the correct values may change during the application testing process.

For a new application implementation, a backup of the target data structures with the configuration and reference data appropriate for the first day of production application processing ("day zero" data) should be kept and retrieved for the start of each round of conversion and application testing. If some or all of the master data is being converted manually, this master data may be part of the "day zero" set of data that is retrieved for the start of each testing cycle. Lookup tables or transformation mapping tables may also be included in this data set.

Testing and dependencies

Tests of data conversion are done independently as well as in conjunction with application testing. Each section and type of data being converted is tested independently, after which types of data should be tested together and finally all conversion data tested together. There may be timing requirements and dependencies from the existing production application system from which the data is being sourced or from the target application system into which data is being loaded. Is there a break in the production process of the systems while conversion is being performed? If not, what is the process if the conversion needs to be rolled back or fails?

If possible, data conversion should populate the environment used in application testing for as many types of testing as possible. The list of types of application testing includes unit testing, integration testing, quality assurance (QA) testing, and end-user testing. There may be additional types of testing, special conversion testing, or QA and end-user testing may be combined.

Business users will sometimes not recognize application functionality as being correct or incorrect without their own data. Therefore, it is particularly important to be using converted data by the time real business users participate in testing. It is a good idea to integrate data conversion and application testing before first-time business users participate in testing; this will eliminate as many issues as possible prior to their involvement. The last round of user acceptance testing prior to production conversion must be prefaced by a full data conversion test and sign-off by the business users.

Private data

In some cases, the developers or application support staff for the target application, or even for the data conversion, are not allowed to see some of the production data for security purposes. Possibly, associated with the source data, there may already exist a set of test data that has been scrubbed or masked of sensitive or private data that can be used for data conversion testing. If scrubbed source data doesn't already exist, then an additional track needs to be added to create scrubbed source data for data conversion and application testing. The development of requirements for data scrubbing of test data needs to be included in the requirements phase and approved by authorized security staff and business owners of the source data. However, it is risky not to be using production data in the early stages of data conversion testing; hopefully, the scrubbed data used for testing is full volume and created from recent production data. It is even riskier not to perform profiling on actual production data during the analysis phase. If at all possible, profiling should be performed on production data by analysts with appropriate access authority. If profiling is not allowed to be performed on production data, this should be listed as a project risk and mitigation steps should be considered.

The final phases of data conversion testing and final user acceptance testing with converted data will need to use unscrubbed data, as well as the production data conversion. Plans should be made for adequate support of the source and target data structures during final testing with staff authorized to gain access to the sensitive data.

Proving

Along with developing the conversion process and code, data conversion must include a process for proving that the conversion is correct. Proof of the data conversion should be entirely independent of the data conversion itself, using none of the same code. Proving processes should be developed for each section of data and an overall proof for the entire data conversion. Where possible, the overall proving process should use financial data for performing the proving.

Data conversion proving is best performed by comparing application financial reports generated from the source and target systems. This would usually be reports of current financial balances that could be compared between the two systems. Best practice is to use actual application reports from the source and target applications for proving whenever available.

Master data conversions may have to be proven by counts of the number of instances in the source and target data structures. Events, transactions, and balances may be proven by both the counts of instances and a sum of numeric fields of both financial and nonfinancial types (such as inventory counts). A financial proof is usually performed for each customer, depending on the nature of the application.

The earlier that the proving process between the two systems is planned and developed, the earlier in the development process that incorrect assumptions and mistakes can be corrected. Most data conversions that leave proving out of planning or leave it until the last minute encounter significant unexpected delays in the production conversion.

Environments

Having sufficient environments for application testing as well as conversion testing is always a challenge, and it will seem that every person on the project is asking for a separate test environment and cannot possibly share. From the start of the project, coordinating testing will be important.

Figure 8.1 shows a possible configuration of environments during application and conversion development. Application developers will want to have environments for both unit testing and integrated system testing. It is usually possible to coordinate a single test environment for both unit and integrated system testing. Depending on how application testing is organized, there may be a request for separate environments for QA testing from user acceptance testing. However, this can usually be coordinated

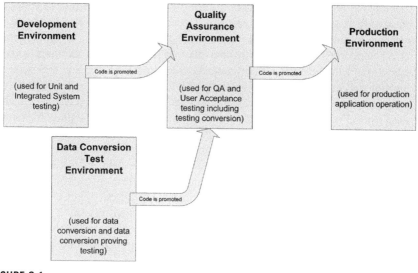

FIGURE 8.1

Environments Data Flow.

to form one environment that can be used for different testing during different phases of the project. At least two test environments usually exist separately from the production environment after the application has been turned on for production operation: the unit/system testing environment (sometimes called development) and the QA/user acceptance testing environment. Since these environments are needed on a permanent basis, they are usually included in the project estimates.

Data conversion testing usually requires at least one separate environment from development and QA. In fact, data conversion testing probably needs one environment for data conversion testing and another environment for data conversion proving testing. Let's assume that the two data conversion development streams (conversion and proving) can coordinate their testing and coexist. It is still very difficult to coordinate all the data conversion testing with the application testing and limit environment needs to the two application test environments (development and QA). It is usually most efficient to have a separate environment for full-volume data conversion testing, if at all possible. When a separate environment is not possible for data conversion, it may be possible to coordinate the project plan so that data conversion testing occurs slightly upstream of application testing: While unit and integrated system testing are occurring in the development environment, data conversion testing occurs in the QA environment. In the case where a new application system is being implemented, it may be possible to continue data conversion and proving testing in the production environment (which is not yet turned on), while QA and user acceptance testing is occurring in the QA environment.

Using cloud resources for temporary testing environments can relieve some of the pressure for extra environment resources. Depending on the location and security of the cloud resources, it may be better to put the unit and system testing environments on temporary cloud resources and the conversion testing on more secure resources, eliminating the extra environment(s) when in production and moving unit and integrated system (development) testing back to the permanent environment.

Business user application testing usually occurs in multiple cycles, each starting with a reset of the application data store and population by data conversion. Changes to software code and configuration may be planned to occur only at the start of each testing cycle. Data conversion may be responsible for an initial setting of the data stores with configuration and reference data. Each testing cycle would begin with resetting the target data stores in the test environment with the initial settings of configuration and reference data, followed by an execution of the data conversion to populate the test environment, then by a data conversion proof, and finally by the execution of the application testing scenarios scheduled for the cycle. Problems with the data conversion or application are logged and addressed in the respective code and process.

Agile development uses short cycles of development and testing, called scrums, to ensure that application code is developed efficiently to meet what business users actually want and need. Whether multiple scrums or just one scrum is scheduled before production implementation, data conversion development, testing, and proving must be part of the agile development team in order to stay coordinated.

A SIDEBAR FROM THE AUTHOR . . . ON DATA CONVERSION

I have spent too many of my weekends during my career doing data conversions or data conversion dress rehearsals. Some might say one is too many, but I found myself with an expertise after a while, and so I would get called in to apply my skills to subsequent data conversion planning and execution.

During one data warehouse project, a data architect who was responsible for designing and managing the data conversion financial proving process, started her analysis extremely early in the project and discovered a myriad of unexpected information about the source systems and the data that she was trying to use to perform the financial proof. Most interestingly, there had been times in the history of the accounting system when the system had made mistakes. The system had been fixed and adjusting accounting entries had been made in the system, but at a higher organizational level than we were using as input to our data warehouse. Therefore, the data in the source system at the level to which we were supposed to prove was incorrect and would never match. The information that the data architect identified by designing and prototyping the financial data proving process prior to the data warehouse code development probably saved us months of delay that would have been caused if we had started the data conversion design later in the project life cycle. The moral of this story is that it is never too early to start designing and developing the conversion proving process. The earlier issues are identified, the smaller the negative impact it will have on the overall project schedule.

When developing a data conversion financial proving process, early in the project you will probably ask the lead business user the question: "What if we find that the information in the source system that we are attempting to prove to is incorrect? Do you want us to prove to the source system or to what is correct?" They will answer "What is correct." This is not true. You will need to prove to the source system AND what is correct, in some way.

Data Archiving

What is data archiving?

What we don't currently emphasize greatly in data management is the end of the data life cycle, when data is archived and, possibly later, deleted. This has been the case because we've wanted to have available as much data as our technical solutions could store and if we couldn't store all of it then the oldest data would just be deleted after backup. Now, in the era of big data, there is exponential growth in the amount of data being produced and the ability to move data aside and retrieve it is more important. Also, and maybe more importantly, it is being discovered that data backups are not sufficient for archiving solutions since they usually don't allow selective retrieval and they lose validity when the live data structures change or applications and technology stacks retire.

Archiving data assumes that the data is moved to a less costly (and possibly less accessible) platform from which it can be retrieved or accessed in the future—either brought back to the original application for access or possibly accessed within the archive environment.

Data archiving is an important area of concern for all organizations, but it is particularly important for mergers and acquisitions, system consolidations, and application replacement. It is important for all data conversions where some data is not being converted to the new environment, especially in heavily regulated industries.

Archiving is heavily utilized with unstructured data, such as e-mail and documents, where there are huge volumes of materials that usually are less likely to be required for access as they become older but for which there may not be a deletion policy. Archiving and retrieval capabilities are frequently built in to e-mail and document management systems, and there are also third-party tools that focus on unstructured data types.

Selecting data to archive

Identifying what data needs to be archived is usually done automatically based on an organizational policy that incorporates any regulatory requirements. Selection criteria may have to do with the age of the data, either when it was created or, more likely, the last time it was updated or accessed. Regulatory requirements may specify the minimal time that data is maintained. For example, consumer loan information must be available for seven years after a loan is rejected or completed, which may require that data be archived if the organizational policy is to keep that data online for less time.

Once the appropriate policy is identified for a data set, the selection and archiving of the appropriate data is usually scheduled to be performed automatically by the archiving system. As with all automated business rules, the archival rules should be reviewed by the business area that is responsible for the data to be in synch with the organizational and regulatory policies. The rules should then be tested to ensure that the appropriate data is being archived.

Can the archived data be retrieved?

Regulatory requirements in many industries, such as pharmaceutical companies, mandate that data from an application being shut down be archived, along with the application code and hardware on which it runs. This is a very intelligent approach to recoverability, since a simple data backup is not recoverable if the hardware that it ran on is no longer available. Less strict regulation may simply require that the data itself be retrievable. Standard data backup capabilities can move the data to offline storage, but bringing the data back into the operational application can be problematic if the structure or schema of the data in the application changes after the data is archived. The structure of data even from the same original data structure or table might change over time, and archived data taken from the same application at various times might be incompatible.

A comprehensive archiving solution should be able to retrieve data even if the application data structures have changed since or even if the application is no longer available.

Conforming data structures in the archiving environment

Archived data is usually placed in storage that is less expensive than the data involved in real-time transaction processing applications, is less speedy, and is usually in a compressed format.

When the archived data only needs to be accessible and does not need to be brought back into the operational application environment, it may be useful to transform the data being archived into a common technical format. It may be decided to store all the data in the data archive environment in the same database management system, for example.

However, trying to create a single logical data model in the data archive environment and to transform the archive data into that format is both cost prohibitive and extremely risky. While it is appropriate for an enterprise data warehouse to be able to report and analyze organizational data using a single logical data model or for an enterprise service bus to be able to move data around an organization, it can be very expensive and has very different goals than archiving. Also, the transformation of the data from its original form to that of the model in the archive environment could produce errors and loss of some of the data's meaning.

Flexible data structures

It is critical that data being archived be done so along with the associated metadata, that explains the meaning of the data and its history.

When archiving data that may have to be accessed independently of the application from which it came, it may be best to use a data structure or storage solution that can both keep the data with can be metadata and allow flexible and changing data structures. An XML type of solution allows for a changing data structure, associated metadata, and still permits queries across data that had been archived from the same application—even if the source data structures had changed.

A SIDEBAR FROM THE AUTHOR ... ON DATA ARCHIVING

I worked on a project in which a retail bank had purchased other banks in the United States. They wanted to consolidate their operations onto one set of application programs and had selected the systems they would use per product. Not all the historical data was to be converted to the core applications, but regulatory requirements, as well as customer service requirements, specified that the data from the applications to be retired needed to be maintained for quite a few more years. Although I proposed copying the historical data to data structures that mirrored those of the applications to be retired, management chose to transform the data to a common logical model in a central new database.

My original proposal was probably not optimal because of the requirement that multiple technologies be maintained to store the archived data. It is preferable to have a single archive solution with all the data accessible. On the other hand, even traditional business intelligence solutions can access data from multiple relational database management systems, so accessing the data from multiple database management systems should not have been a particular challenge.

The problems with transforming the data into a common logical model are twofold: First, it is a *very* big project to define a common logical model and map various data structures to it; and second, errors may be introduced in the transformation that are not detected until long after the data archiving when the data needs to be retrieved. As anyone who has worked on an enterprise data warehouse project can vouch, creating a central common data model is a difficult and time-consuming task. Additionally, mapping data from its original structure to a common central structure is difficult and time consuming. Unless it is central to the success of a data project, such as an enterprise data warehouse or master data management application, it is best practice to avoid creating and mapping to a central logical data model.

It is generally agreed that it is best to archive data in its original logical structure using a technology that keeps the metadata with the data and can handle variations in data structures, such as an XML or JSON solution. Data can be accessed and integrated in one technical solution, with little risk of losing some of the original data content.

INTERVIEW WITH AN EXPERT: JOHN ANDERSON ON DATA ARCHIVING AND DATA INTEGRATION

Following is an interview with John Anderson on the importance and use of data integration in data archiving.

John Anderson is an enterprise system project manager and architect with more than 14 years of professional experience in information systems management and development in the Life Sciences and Financial Services industries. He has worked on a large number of enterprise archiving projects throughout these industries as both architect and manager.

How is data integration (i.e., moving and transforming data) related to data archiving?

My approach to archiving has always been to analyze the usage for the data and from that analysis create scenarios for archiving based on risk, compliance, needs for data access, costs, and value. These scenarios then naturally devolve into larger categories of archiving patterns. A key part of most of these patterns (with perhaps the exception of "Live" archiving) is extract, transform, and load (ETL) activities. ETL work in larger projects is often the long pole in the tent, from a project management standpoint: These activities often take the longest time to complete and are the most-error prone, all while being the most essential.

The definition of archiving boils down to something like the following: "Archiving is the storage, searching, and retrieval of digital content." Among its many uses, archiving serves as an aid to the migration of systems and data, for the preservation of intellectual property; to improve system health and performance; and to support litigation and other legal requirements. Simply put, the three corners of archiving (storage, searching, and retrieval) don't occur without data integration; there is always a source and target system.

How and why is data moved for data archiving?

The how is often the bigger question, but we won't forget about the why.

Data is usually moved from source system to target archive through some ETL platform and/or data-dumping mechanism from an underlying database structure. In cases of unstructured data migration, data stored in files, which may be in coded form (e.g., Microsoft Office) or noncoded, pictorial form (e.g., scanned TIF images), data of the underlying operating system or storage system are used as the key for tagging and tracking the data. In many cases, simple OS copy utilities can be utilized. The key, however, to any data moving for archiving relies heavily on two of the three corners of archiving mentioned earlier: searching and retrieval. Data moved without the ability to be appropriately indexed and retrieved is useless.

I have seen many an archiving project spend countless hours migrating terabytes upon terabytes of useless data. What's important to understand as a part of the ETL or migration activities is how the data will be used in an archived state and what is actually required to be kept.

This discussion moves us along to the why part of the question. In my opinion it is vital to understand why data is being archived. Many companies have taken a "keep it all" strategy. At first glance this can seem to be a viable option because who can understand what the future may hold, and nowadays disk (i.e., storage) is relatively cheap. However, experience has taught us that from a liability standpoint, and sometimes from a regulatory standpoint, storing more data than is required is not the best business choice. Often older data may open a company up to legal exposure that was not necessary given legal, regulatory, and often even the own company's retention policies. As part of my own personal methodology for archiving, any target application or source of data needs to pass the "Why archive?" question. I need to understand what legal, regulatory, and business practices mandate that this data be held onto. That analysis all comes down to does it save or make money, keep us compliant (i.e., out of jail), or significantly increase efficiency. Once those issues are understood and evaluated, then archiving can proceed.

What kinds of transformations are done to the data being archived? (e.g., compression, different data structures, etc.)

Any number of transformations may be done on data that is being archived, depending on the archiving platform. Typically, at a minimum, some type of compression can be applied to the underlying data store after the data has quiesced. Sometimes this compression is done through manual effort from archiving tools or the underlying hardware itself through complicated compression algorithms and disk striping methodologies.

Another common transformation that occurs in archiving, regardless of industry, is the transformation to a durable format. A durable format could be a number of things from the media standards use to store the data (i.e., WORM, COLD media types, optical disk, etc.) or the actual format of the data that is being stored being encapsulated or snapshotted to XML or PDF. The latter two format changes seem to reflect the most common trend in archiving, as they are industry recognized as more standard and relatable formats. The use of XML encapsulation/transformation and its self-describing nature has resulted in the usage of a wide number of archiving tools that leverage XML databases as opposed to typical relational databases.

How is data integration for data archiving different from backup and recovery?

Archiving is concerned with preserving the data and information stored in the system and not necessarily the source system itself. The format data may have in an archive may not be a mirror image of the "application context" it had in the source system.

How is data archiving for structured data (i.e., relational databases and XML) different from data archiving for unstructured data?

The primary difference is actually in the data analysis and the tools. As stated earlier, two of the key parts of archiving are search and retrieval of the data. Structured data, whether XML or relational databases, are especially designed for that searching and retrieving. Unstructured data by its nature is free form. Typically, the only way to search and index this data is full-text indexing, which involves a whole other level of complexity as well, to ensure that whatever tools or code being developed can read the variety of unstructured content that exist in your source systems (multiple office formats, PDFs, texts, spreadsheets, proprietary databases and images). Images can pose a particular set of issues, given the huge variety of formats and encapsulation techniques used. I recall projects in which we could not move forward with archiving purely because we were dealing with a variety of imaging formats and had to develop specific code to deal with this variety.

Have you seen any data archiving projects where data integration issues led to significant problems?

Absolutely. By data integration I am referring to the ETL process. Often in archiving projects, the ETL from legacy systems has presented problems. In one situation I recall that my team was trying to extract data from a legacy mainframe system that was built around ADABAS. Some of the constructs specific to Natural programming and ADABAS presented significant issues to our ETL process. The programming construct that basically provided dynamic duplication of code pages and values was a nightmare to convert to a more easily understood format. We would often end up with thousands of blank fields of data as the ETL process tried to interpret empty arrays and data structures based purely on their dimension as opposed to actually utilized elements.

Have you had experiences where data integration was neglected on a data archiving project?

Yes. I have worked on projects in which the idea was simply to get the data out of the active applications and into archive repository. Typically, these projects are those that deal with semistructured or unstructured report-type data with well-understood attributes or a common format. In these projects, the ability to just dump the system into some type of content management repository made the archiving relatively straightforward since the ECM system provided some level of full-text indexing and allowed more robust searching.

What kind of issues can arise with data recoverability from archive?

Data that cannot be easily retrieved from the archive is essentially useless. Often the business case around archiving is built around return on investment (ROI) from decommissioning redundant and legacy systems and being able to respond to legal discovery concerns. If the archived data is not readily recoverable, then its use from a discovery standpoint is limited, given the time constraints on legal matters

What do you think about transforming data into a common format in the archive, either a common technology or a common schema? Have you had any problems with this in the past?

The creation of a durable archive format is the intent of any good archiving system. Transformation to that format, and in fact determining that format, is the rub. The format types have changed over the years. When first being involved with archiving back in the early 1990s everything was about WORM drives and optical disks as the format that would last forever. There was no concern for the data form, but the media format became the focus. Only later did people begin to realize that the media format was not as durable as originally thought, and if you don't change the data format you now need to mothball these old systems in order to read the format.

What kinds of tools or technologies are used to support data integration for data archiving?

The technologies include ETL tools and platforms, scripting languages (such as Perl), OS-related command tools, XML utilities, converters, and parsers. The key aspect of all of these tools is the driver for the multitude of databases and data formats that exist. I have had more than one project sidelined because the tools we chose could not handle a certain type of database well or efficiently.

Are the tools for data archiving different for structured and unstructured data?

Yes, one of the key areas for archiving structured data is data analysis. To ensure that archive users can get to what they need, you need to understand the data you are archiving to ensure that archive users can get to what they need. This lends itself to any variety of database toolsets that do entity relationship diagramming and more complex data analysis. Now that's all well and good for structured data where you have some tool set to easily navigate, but when dealing with images and other types of unstructured and semistructured your primary tools are going to be focused on being able to inject more order and structure into the data. Unstructured data analysis tools now look at patterns on the objects and text in the objects as well as where the file is stored, who last accessed it, what location it is in, the file name, size, and so on. It becomes more of a forensic science than just interrogating the data itself.

How do you think the area of data archiving is changing? Where do you think this area is going to?

Most companies are focusing on portfolio rationalization, often resulting in data/application archiving as an offset driven primarily by regulatory compliance needs. Forrester Research estimates that, on average, structured data repositories for large applications grow by 50 percent annually and that 85 percent of data stored in databases is inactive.

Do you think the technologies for performing data archiving, especially around data integration, are changing?

Yes. Varying types of data warehouses (containing both structured and unstructured data) are in evidence, as are a move toward XML-based databases for use in the archive and the use of other nonrelational data stores.

Batch Data Integration Architecture and Metadata

INFORMATION IN THIS CHAPTER

What is batch data integration architecture?

In order to enable batch data integration, it is necessary to have the tools to support analysis and development of the data integration code as well as the tools to support the operation of the data integration activities.

Some tools can provide multiple functions. This is a very mature area of data management, and some of the available tools are extremely sophisticated: They are able to handle very high volumes, fast load times, and extremely complex transformations, with operational data movement, transformation, and scheduling built in. Very complex capabilities come with a relatively high price tag and the need to be operated by specialists who are experts in using the tools. Most medium to large organizations invest in a sophisticated batch data integration capability for at least one area of need, such as loading the data warehouses and data marts. Figure 10.1 shows the tools and systems needed to implement a batch data integration capability.

Profiling tool

A profiling tool is important for performing analysis of the source and target data structures for data integration, whether the transformation will be performed in a

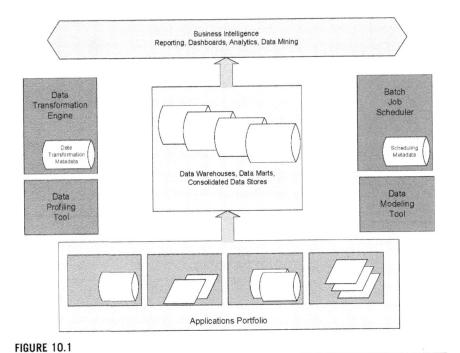

FIGURE 10.1

Batch Data Integration Architecture.

batch or real-time environment. It is possible to perform profiling using just the utilities of the source data environment, but specialized profiling tools make the analysis process much more efficient, especially on large volumes of data. Some data-profiling tools can actually infer the relationships between data based on the actual data contents of the various data structures. Basic metadata tools can infer relationships between the data based on the names of the fields or attributes in the data structures.

Modeling tool

Modeling may be needed for the intermediate staging and file layouts, not just the source and target data structures. The most efficient use of resources is to develop robust models that can be reused for multiple functions, such as data file layouts that can be used for multiple data conversions or for loading data into the data warehouse from multiple sources. Modeling tools should be able to model interface and file layouts as well as operational data structures, such as databases. In addition to data modeling, process modeling tools may be needed to design the flow of data between applications.

Metadata repository

Most of the tools listed for use in data integration will have their own underlying metadata repository. One benefit of an integrated tool that performs multiple functions needed for data integration is that it is probably using the same metadata repository across those functions. This is not always the case, however, as a tool might be using different repositories for different purposes. Sometimes a vendor will buy a tool to perform a function that is missing from its current set of capabilities, or to perform it better, and multiple metadata repositories may be functioning in the background. All tools that act on data in the organization, including database management systems and document management systems, work with a specialized metadata repository that contains information on the data under management.

There are three basic categories of metadata: business, technical, and operational. Business metadata is the information of particular interest to business users and was probably developed by business people, such as the business definitions of terms associated with data. Technical metadata is the information that is needed for the programs to function, such as the technical name of a field in a database or the calculation that needs to occur to transform a piece of data from one format to another. Operational metadata is the log of what actually occurred, such as the date and time that a particular piece of data was loaded into the target data structure.

There is metadata about every layer of the technical environment and its use: network, servers, databases, files, programs, as well as who is allowed to access all these different layers. For data integration, there are some new pieces of metadata that are particularly of interest: data transformation information and lineage. Data transformation metadata is the information about how data from one environment should be transformed to another. The common term for data transformation is *mapping*. Mapping is both a noun and a verb. It is the act of defining what the data transformation should be, and the resulting specification of this transformation is also called the mapping. Lineage is the history of where data came from and how it was transformed along the way. Lineage information is operational metadata about the source of data. Lineage metadata presents an inherent challenge because it is based on the technical metadata mappings that were performed on the data, and although it is of great interest to business users, it tends to be incomprehensible. It is usually necessary to create additional business metadata that explains in business terms the lineage of data.

Data movement

Some tool is needed to move data from location to location, between servers or networks or organizations. Utilities specialized for different environments or a special tool that handles multiple environments and any physical data storage transformation might be used. The data movement tool may require sophisticated security capabilities as well, if passing data between organizations.

Transformation

Data transformation can be extremely simple or extremely complex. It is necessary to develop the data transformation, or mapping, instructions. The tools for developing transformation code provide options for the various types of transformation categories, whether one is simply moving the data from one field to another or one needs to merge data from multiple sources and look up how values from the source should be transformed to valid values in the target. Usually the transformation development tools have sophisticated user interfaces. The more complex the tool capabilities, the more likely the need to involve specialist programmers for the transformation development who are experts in using that tool. Vendors may show demonstrations that appear to be very easy and may indicate that business people who are not programmers can use the data transformation tool, but this is not realistic.

The data transformation development tool will store the metadata about the transformation in the metadata repository. Either the transformation tool will generate the code that can be executed to perform the transformation, or it will perform the operational transformation itself. Some data transformation tools are complex operational systems that execute the transformations using the stored mapping metadata as instructions in how to transform the data. These operational transformation engines are designed to handle very high volumes of data transformations at very high speeds. The operational transformation engines (or data integration engines) are designed exactly for this function and can be tuned with professional advice to be extremely efficient. Most organizations use a data transformation engine for batch data integration.

Operational transformation engines have a few drawbacks that should be considered when designing the batch data transformation architecture: If the engine isn't working, the data transformation can't be performed; the organizational needs may be much simpler than the capabilities of the tool; and the organization may have the need for even greater speed than the operational engine can provide. Adding a data transformation operational engine may raise the cost of operating the data transformation environment because the technical specialists must be available to support any problems that occur in the execution of the data transformation. If the engine is down, the execution can't occur, so the engine must become part of the set of applications that require immediate problem resolutions even in the middle of the night.

If the need for batch data transformation is rather simple, running the data transformation engine may be the most complex and costly aspect of operating the environment, and batch data transformation could be performed more efficiently using generated code. Very rarely, organizations with extremely complex batch data transformation needs sometimes find that they cannot tune the data transformation operational engines to be sufficiently fast for their needs. Further, they will find that they are able to tune data transformations using code that can be compiled and other alternative approaches to meet their batch data transformation time limitations. The very few organizations that have more complex data transformation needs than can be handled by the standard transformation engines will probably be investing in a custom solution, which is more expensive than the cost of purchase and operation of the vendor transformation engines.

For various reasons, as listed earlier, batch data transformation is sometimes performed using code generated from the data transformation tool, or it can be hand written, which can then be compiled and executed. This arrangement may suit organizations that have few and simple data transformation needs or vastly complex and difficult data transformation needs, the two ends of the spectrum. Not having a data transformation engine in the operational environment makes the environment much simpler, but requires greater manual care of the metadata and scheduling. A data transformation engine will generate lineage metadata that is unlikely to be otherwise available, unless particularly programmed.

Scheduling

Many organizations have standard scheduling tools for executing batch operations. Data transformation engines have their own scheduling capabilities or schedules that can be invoked from a standard scheduler. Code generated from a data transformation tool or custom code can be executed by a scheduler.

Most organizations prefer to have their batch data transformation triggered from their standard scheduler as part of the integrated "nightly" batch processing for the entire organization. Much of the data to be extracted from the organization's application systems and transformed is dependent on being at a particular "state" in the processing cycle. Each application may have a certain amount of batch processing that needs to occur before the data in the application reaches the correct state ready to be extracted. By running all batch processing from the same scheduler, any dependencies between systems can be automated into the schedule. Also, an organization may prefer to have all schedules run from the same scheduler so that production support of the schedules can be performed and managed centrally using resources trained on one standard set of tools.

For organizations that don't have a standard scheduler and don't run and support a centralized production schedule, batch data transformation tools provide a scheduler. It is necessary to establish a trigger from each application, providing data to the batch data transformation to indicate when the data is "done" or in the proper state and ready for extract.

A SIDEBAR FROM THE AUTHOR ... ON BATCH DATA INTEGRATION METADATA

My advice is to take everything you read (as in existing metadata) or hear about the contents of data structures with a grain of salt. I have created many data dictionaries that provide definitions of the business terms in an organization and usually that map to the actual database fields where this data can be found. When I was a consultant, and therefore not an employee of the organization in question, I found it very difficult to get permission to get access to the actual production data in question, so I was generating these definitions by looking at the field names, checking existing metadata about the field, and talking to business users and technologists who support the data. I tried to warn clients that the probability of these definitions and mappings being wholly correct was remote. Yet, I ended creating data definitions frequently with little idea about what was actually being stored in the data structures. Thus, future analysts would read the metadata I had generated and possibly assume that it was correct. A colleague of mine used to say that anything learned about a piece of data before actually looking at it was just rumor, and my experience has been that what is found in a production data environment contains unexpected results almost every time. Data contents are frequently null or blank, contain all defaults, or present entirely different information than the field name would lead you to believe. Once again, I am suggesting that data profiling is absolutely crucial to data-oriented projects.

A SIDEBAR FROM THE AUTHOR ... ON METADATA REPOSITORIES

Every tool and data structure technology has an underlying metadata repository for its associated configuration and, at least, technical metadata. However, data projects frequently seek to consolidate metadata into a single repository in order to be able to analyze and report on the metadata across types and regarding relationships and lineage, and so on. Depending on the organization and analysis need, the return on investment for a metadata repository project can be very compelling. But the investment required to purchase and implement a central metadata repository can be very high, close to or over one million dollars. The first time I assessed the market in central metadata repositories, in the late 1990s, I decided that the players were too new and didn't have sufficient functionality to make an investment at that time and for that project, a data warehouse project, a good choice. Instead we used the tool repository from the ETL tool for the analysis and reporting needs.

Years later, when I again needed to assess metadata repositories, I found that the maturity of the market had not significantly changed from my previous analysis. In fact, it seemed that most of the vendors were entirely different except for a couple players. The top tools had developed compatibility with more types of metadata, but the market still seemed immature and the top solutions sometimes were in near obsolete technology platforms.

The big advance in centralized metadata has come from the leadership in metadata standardization, especially from the Object Modeling Group (OMG), a consortium focused on modeling and model-based standards. Since OMG has identified common formats for the expression of metadata, central metadata repository vendors can more efficiently build integration with various tool repositories without having to deal with myriad proprietary data structures.

Vendors of central metadata repositories are selling very robust and effective products these days. Central metadata repository implementation projects are very much like data warehouse projects, where metadata from various source systems or tools are fed into a central repository. Be careful on entering into such a project, however, and make sure there is a very concrete expression of exactly what will be gained from the project, as they are notoriously expensive with strangely elusive return on investment.

INTERVIEW WITH AN EXPERT: ADRIENNE TANNENBAUM ON METADATA AND DATA INTEGRATION

Following is an interview with Adrienne Tannenbaum on the importance and use of metadata in data integration.

Adrienne Tannenbaum has specialized in metadata aspects of IT since 1994 when Microsoft partnered with Texas Instruments to architect the first metadata repository. She is a recognized leading expert on metadata and the author of two books on the subject: *Implementing a Corporate Repository* (Wiley, 1994) and *Metadata Solutions* (Addison-Wesley, 2002). She is a frequent conference speaker and author of many articles in various technical publications.

How is data integration (i.e., moving and transforming data) related to metadata?
Moving and transforming data, from one source to another, is based on an underlying metamodel, which describes the physical structure of each source. Simply speaking the "data" is described by "content" in a metamodel, and this "content" depicts the full transformation story.

What kind of metadata is kept regarding data movement and transformation (business, technical, operational)?
All of the above. In order to move data, we need to know the source (technical), we need to know what it means (business), what will happen to it (business and technical), and where it is going (technical). The process of getting it from one place to another is operational.

Have you seen any data integration projects where metadata issues led to significant problems?
Virtually every project that I have worked on has failed to give the right amount of emphasis to "business" metadata." Even when the technical metadata is complete, it is not associated with sufficient business metadata such as classifications and business rules, and is therefore misunderstood by the most important people—the business owners— the people who need and use the data that is being integrated.

Have you had experiences where particular attention was paid to metadata for data integration?
I always emphasize the need to capture the business aspects of all data integration efforts. For example, most ETL tools do not require "descriptions" to be associated with the transformation logic, but a good analyst makes sure that those fields are populated.

Have you had experiences where metadata was neglected on a data integration project?
Always. I have yet to work on a data integration effort where the metadata aspects were not neglected. Most project participants do not realize the value since they are convinced that everyone else has the same knowledge base that they do regarding the data itself.

If some already know the answers, they can't understand why they should take the time to document the answers. I always hear about not having time, or being under a tight deadline, and so on.

What kinds of tools or technologies are used to support data integration metadata?

ETL tools have fields such as "definition" and "description" which can be used to capture the "business" aspects of data integration metadata. Of course, the metamodel for each tool has the ability to keep the metadata, which covers the full integration picture (business, technical, operational).

Centralized metadata repositories support all types of metadata and are able to integrate specific aspects of "integration" metadata with the details that may already exist in the repository with respect to the sources and targets, as well as the business metadata that surrounds the entire lineage.

And of course, unfortunately, the most popular tool that supports data integration metadata is an Excel spreadsheet.

Do you think there should be a central metadata repository in addition to having data integration metadata in the separate tool repositories? Why or why not?

Central repositories contain the only view that is enterprise focused. Data integration is based on sources that are already in existence, and perhaps are also being used for other "integration efforts." Unless one integration effort is aware of another integration effort, an organization runs the risk of what I call the "batch in–batch out" architecture. Unless there is one view across the organization, no one will really know what is going on with major data sources—even if they are well documented for a major data transformation effort.

Are there special considerations around the movement of metadata for data integration into a central metadata repository or into a data warehouse? Are there other places that data integration metadata is needed?

Every source needs to be named consistently so that the same source is not identified twice. But physical sources are typically "scanned" into central repositories, and this issue is resolved based on their identification within a database management system (DBMS) catalog. Problems can arise with manual identification, such as when sourcing information from a spreadsheet.

How is data integration of unstructured data different from that of structured data?

Unstructured data is integrated with structured data by association of both types of data with a fixed classification or taxonomy.

How do you think the area of metadata is changing? Where do you think this area is going to?

Metadata is no longer being considered an "area." Instead it is a recognized characteristic of life within IT. The concepts are now becoming "governance" concepts and are more related to metadata content, when it should be populated, why, how, and what valid values should be used.

Do you think the technologies for metadata, especially around data integration, are changing?

Metadata itself is becoming more of an automated capture. The business side of metadata will always require manual intervention of sorts, at some point on the timeline. At best, keyword searches can make best guesses as to how data should be identified or categorized, but the definitions and associations will always require a person.

Real Time Data Integration

Introduction to Real-Time Data Integration

Why real-time data integration?

For most data integration requirements, overnight, batch data movement is simply no longer acceptable. It is not acceptable to be unable to see the results of a business transaction until the next day. Nor is it any longer acceptable for a customer to open an account with an organization but be unable to transact the same day.

Real-time data interactions usually have limitations on the amount or size of the data that can be involved in one interaction. The term for the block of data involved in one real-time interaction is referred to as a "message." On the other hand, there are few limits on the size of data involved in a batch interaction. It is also necessary for each real-time interaction message to traverse all the levels of security described for batch interaction, but since this needs to occur for each smaller set of data, or message, real-time data movement tends to be slower for large volumes of data than batch data movement. In some types of applications, the volume-handling capabilities of batch data integration are advantageous and lend themselves to a batch approach to data movement, but most data integration activity is now performed real time or close to real time.

Real-time interactions between application systems are usually called interfaces, the same term that is used for the batch interactions between application systems. The portfolio of applications to be managed by an organization, which can be daunting for even medium-sized organizations that have only hundreds of distinct active applications, can sometimes be overwhelmed by the complexity of managing the interfaces needed between the applications.

The technology for handling real-time data integration is slightly more complicated than that for batch data integration. The basic activities of extract, transform, and load are still present, but of course, they are occurring real time and at a business transaction level.

Managing real-time interfaces between each application or "point to point" is significantly less efficient than managing the set of all necessary interactions between applications in a portfolio, as will be explained in this chapter. Therefore, it is critical that every organization have an enterprise data integration architecture and management capability, for attempting to manage interfaces without it can quickly become overwhelmingly complex.

Why two sets of technologies?

Is it necessary for an organization to have both batch and real-time data integration tools? Why not just have the one set of tools that can handle real-time integration and then use the same toolset and engine to load the batched data on the necessary schedule? Why pay for two sets of technology licenses and two sets of experts to code the transformations and support the interfaces?

The first reason for keeping the batch integration capability after creating a real-time data integration capability is that the existing batch interfaces are written, tested, and in production. Moving the interfaces to another technology would be a substantial cost in time and resources. Change might be cost justified in not having to maintain licenses on two sets of technologies and pay for two sets of technical experts.

It turns out, however, that the ultimate reason for needing to maintain two sets of technologies for both batch and real-time data integration is that usually the speed at which real-time data integration works is insufficient to process the volumes of transactions in a normal batch data interface window available for loading a data warehouse or even to complete a data conversion in the available time period. Real-time data integration is inherently slower because for each piece of information being moved, all the layers of security access need to be invoked and accessed through the application programming interface (API). Changing a data warehouse architecture to load data as data in the source system is changed, rather than daily or weekly, would probably alleviate some of the time pressure, but snapshots of data taken at a particular time (such as end of day) may still be too much volume for a real-time interface to process in the available batch window.

Therefore, most organizations implement the tools for both batch data integration and real-time data integration and use the appropriate tools for the appropriate task. The batch data integration tools are usually owned by the data warehouse applications and are used for any data conversions when it becomes appropriate.

Data Integration Patterns

12

INFORMATION IN THIS CHAPTER

Interaction patterns

Although the area of data integration is seen as purely technical, the most significant best practices are not about technologies but designs and patterns of integration. Certain techniques for managing data in motion have been developed to lessen complexity and allow for change and scalability. These are not technologies but approaches to orchestrating the movement of data that, though possibly not intuitive, provide significant advantages over traditional interface development techniques.

Loose coupling

In designing interactions between applications and organizations, one best practice is to design the connection to be as "loose" as possible. What this implies is that a failure of one system doesn't necessarily mean that both systems fail, and that either system could be replaced without the need to change the remaining system. Traditional real-time interfaces between systems tended to "tightly couple" the systems together, especially in that the code of the interface was specific for the connection between only those two systems, and replacing either usually required rewriting the interface.

Designing loose coupling between systems usually requires the clear definition of an API (application programming interface) for at least one side of the interaction. The API defines exactly how information should be formatted to request a function of that application: to provide information, to store information, or to perform some other operations. This is the equivalent of calling a program procedure or a function. If the APIs of the applications are well defined, then it should be possible to replace either side of the interaction without the need to recode the other side. The emphasis here is that a well-defined interaction process exists but it is not necessary to know anything specific about the technology in which it is implemented.

Loosely coupled interactions tend to be "near real time" rather than real time in that it should be possible for one of the applications to be, at least briefly, unavailable, without both applications being unavailable. Therefore, interactions should be designed not to wait for one another. This is not always possible if an application needs information from another application to proceed or the operation to be performed is a dependency.

Hub and spoke

The most significant and most important design pattern for architecting real-time data integration solutions is the "hub-and-spoke" design for data interactions. This pattern should be used in order to implement real-time data integration for an organization of even medium size; otherwise the interfaces become overly complex and unmanageable.

Traditional interface designs use a "point to point" interface whereby each system directly interacts with each system with which it wants to share data. So, between any two systems that need to share data, at least one interface is designed and built where data from one system is transformed and passed to the other system. This type of interface design is illustrated in Figure 12.1, showing just five applications in the portfolio. The data transformation, as well as the orchestration of when and how the data is passed, must be specified, and then the programs can be written on both sides. If there are two systems that need to share data, then only one interface needs to be written. If there are four systems that all need to share data, then six interfaces between them are needed. The formula for the number of interfaces developed point to point, if the number of systems involved is equal to "n" is (n * (n −1))/2. Thus, if an organization has 10 systems that need to share data, the number of interfaces needed is (10 * (10−1))/2 = 45. If there are 100 systems, then the number of interfaces is (100 * (100−1))/2 = 4950.

This formula is an estimate, since not every system in an organization needs to interface with every other. Usually, however, there needs to be more than one interface between any two systems with different kinds of data to be shared. The

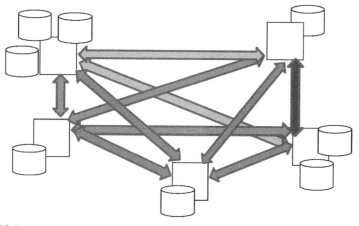

FIGURE 12.1

Exponential Number of Interactions with Point to Point Interfaces.

formula is exponential in nature and the number of interfaces quickly becomes unreasonable. Even medium-sized companies usually have more than 100 systems. The number of interfaces needed for interactions with 1000 systems is almost half a million. Every time a new application is added to the portfolio, interfaces need to be developed to "n" other systems—all the already existing systems in the organization. Figure 12.2 shows the exponential growth in the number of interfaces against the number of applications in an organization's portfolio using point-to-point interfaces.

It is no wonder that most of the complexity in managing a portfolio of applications arises from maintaining the interfaces. As mentioned earlier, the current process of including purchased vendor packages in the application portfolio whenever possible only exacerbates the problem, since every package uses its own set of tables or files that must be kept in synch with those of the rest of the organization.

Modern techniques of data architecture use the creation of central data for master data management, business intelligence, and data warehousing to clarify what the proper source is for particular purposes, but these are not the hubs referred to in "hub and spoke." The data integration technique of hub and spoke is most effective if used for every real-time interaction, but need not replace every existing production interface to help bring the massive complexity of interfaces back to a manageable level. The formula for the number of interfaces needed for "n" systems using the hub-and-spoke model is just "n." Every time a new application is added to the portfolio, only one interface needs to be developed from the new system to the "hub." This technique can potentially change the number of interfaces that an organization needs to manage from an unmanageable

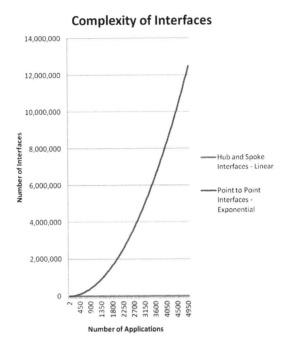

Complexity of Interfaces

FIGURE 12.2

Growth in Number of Interfaces.

exponential number to a much more reasonable linear number. The hub-and-spoke approach to managing interfaces is the most significant process improvement technique and best practice for application portfolio management efficiency. Figure 12.3 depicts how fewer and how much simpler are the interfaces needed for a portfolio of five applications using the hub-and-spoke design approach for interfaces. As shown in Figure 12.2, the number of interfaces using a hub-and-spoke architecture will be linear, equal to the number of applications.

The data interaction "hub" is a technology solution data structure that business users may not be aware of, even if such a structure is running in their organization. The layout of the organization's data is maintained in the hub, but not a repository of data. In other words, all data passing between systems needs to be transformed into the format defined in the hub, but the data is not stored in the hub. In actuality, the transformed data doesn't really go to a central place but is just transformed into a shared format. The format of data in the hub needs to be well thought out and designed to support all the interfaces of data in the organization. The design of the data format in the data hub is usually called a canonical model, because the design of the data hub needs to be the definitive design of the data passed between applications, or the "canon".

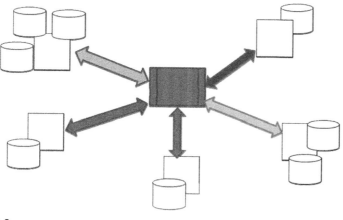

FIGURE 12.3

Linear Number of Interactions with Hub and Spoke Interface Design.

Synchronous and asynchronous interaction

Synchronous interactions are those in which one system sends a message to another and waits for an acknowledgment or response before it proceeds. This type of interaction is common where the first requesting system needs something from the second in order to continue the process, such as further detail on master data or a preference. Clearly, this is a tightly coupled interaction, and both systems must be operational and online in order for the process to be successful.

Asynchronous interactions are those in which the requesting system doesn't wait for an answer to proceed, but continues processing, and doesn't require information back from the second system. Asynchronous interactions may be requesting some action be taken and no response sent back, or a response may be expected eventually and may even assume a response fairly quickly, in fact, but does not sit and wait for it.

Request and reply

A standard interaction model is the request and reply model whereby one system sends a message to another and expects a response back with either the information requested or an acknowledgment that the request was received and the service requested was completed. This interaction may be either synchronous or asynchronous, and it may be direct or through a hub. Figure 12.4 depicts the simple steps of a request and reply interaction.

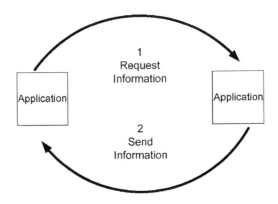

FIGURE 12.4

Request and Reply Interaction.

Publish and subscribe

Another standard interaction model is the publish and subscribe model. Application systems declare their interest in a type or piece of information by "subscribing" to the information in question. Systems that produce or acquire the information of interest will send any new or revised information out to those systems that have previously declared their interest, or "publish" the information to the network of interested systems. Tracking the subscriptions and determining whether the subscribing system has access rights to the particular piece of information may be handled by the publishing system or a separate orchestration system that manages the data interactions.

Two-phase commit

A single business transaction may require updates to be made by multiple applications. It may be critical that either all updates are performed or none, but in no case should only some of the updates be performed, even if some of the applications should fail to complete their assignments. An example would be a bank savings account update: If a deposit comes in, then both the transaction should be logged and the account balance should be updated, but under no circumstances should one activity take place without the other, even if a disaster occurs (such as a power outage).

As shown in Figure 12.5, the two-phase commit transaction involves confirming first that all of the applications involved are prepared to perform their respective updates and second that all of the applications performed them successfully. If any of the applications involved fails to acknowledge that they performed their part of

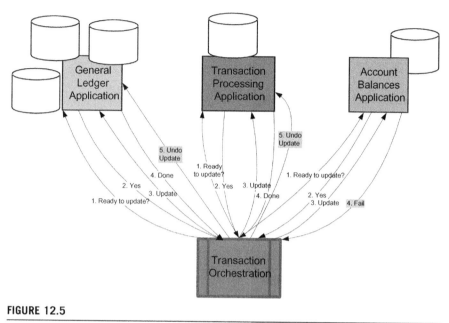

FIGURE 12.5

Two-Phase Commit Transaction Back Out.

the transaction, then all the other applications are instructed to undo, or back out, any of the updates they had made.

Integrating interaction types

It is sometimes necessary to build interactions between systems which have different inherent interaction models. In order to build an interface between a publish and subscribe system and a request and reply system, it may be necessary to create a somewhat complex store and forward solution that stores all the updates made by a publishing system until a request is made for a particular piece of information. Since this is actually creating another copy of the source system or master file, it is probably more efficient to ensure that master data hubs can interact using both the publish and subscribe and the request and reply interaction methods.

Core Real-Time Data Integration Technologies

INFORMATION IN THIS CHAPTER

Confusing terminology

Even some experts in the area of data management use various real-time data integration terminology interchangeably, although these concepts have distinct meanings. Therefore, it is not surprising that those who are not experts find the various shades of meaning somewhat confusing.

In summary, enterprise application integration (EAI) is an approach to integrating or passing data between applications of various technologies, whereas service-oriented architecture (SOA) is an interaction approach for applications that are using a common technical protocol for interfacing or calling to one another. An enterprise service bus (ESB) is the tool most commonly used for EAI. Since most organizations want to integrate at least a few of their legacy applications that use different technology than their newer applications which are usually written using SOA, plus purchased application packages using whatever technology in which they happen to be implemented, most organizations use an ESB for real-time data integration and orchestration. Enterprise information integration (EII) is sometimes used as a synonym for EAI, but it specifically refers to cases where the data underlying an application is being accessed directly for integration rather than access through the application code and services.

Enterprise service bus (ESB)

Central to most real-time data integration solutions, and especially "hub and spoke" solutions, is the implementation of an enterprise service bus. An ESB is an application that usually runs on a separate server from any of the other applications and tools in the organization's portfolio of business applications. Almost all enterprise, operational, real-time, or near real-time data integration solutions use an enterprise service bus. In other words, most data interfaces that happen while the application systems are up and running and supporting daily work are usually implemented using an ESB. Data interfaces focused on getting information to a central hub at the end of daily work, such as a data warehouse, point to point model may use other methods for data integration, such as a batch data integration solution.

An enterprise service bus is used to coordinate the movement of data messages across different servers that may be running different technologies. Figure 13.1 depicts an ESB configuration. Each server (physical or virtual) being connected by the ESB will have an adapter installed on that server and incoming and outgoing message queues for each application. The adapter will handle any transformations that need to occur because of different technologies that are involved in the interface. Therefore, the adapters are specific for the operating system and data structure technologies running on their respective servers.

The enterprise service bus will continuously "poll" every outgoing message queue for each application connected, process any messages found, and put messages on the incoming message queue for any relevant application. If a server is not available, or "down," then the ESB will hold any messages for that server until it is available. If the server is available but an application on the server is

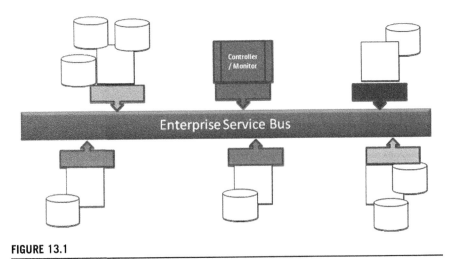

FIGURE 13.1

Enterprise Service Bus.

down, then the messages for that application will sit on the application message queue until the application is back up and picks up the messages.

The implementation of an ESB will usually also include the logical implementation of a hub and spoke interaction model. The application that implements the hub and spoke and transforms any data into the common format (or canonical model) of the hub and then to the specific format of the receiving systems may be co-located with the ESB engine or may be a separate application. Similarly, the software to orchestrate the interactions between the applications may be independent or together with the other coordination components of the ESB. The orchestration software will handle subscriptions by applications showing interest in particular types of information and the subsequent distribution of the relevant information when it is published. The ESB will also need to have a monitoring application for use by a systems administrator to view and manage the data movement of the ESB. Enterprise Service Buses are generally classified as "middleware" as they support the application software across operating systems.

INTERVIEW WITH AN EXPERT: DAVID S. LINTHICUM ON ESB AND DATA INTEGRATION

Following is an interview with David S. Linthicum on the importance and use of ESBs in data integration.

David (Dave) S. Linthicum is the Chief Technology Officer and founder of Blue Mountain Labs. He is an internationally recognized industry expert and thought leader, and the author and coauthor of 13 books on computing, including the best-selling *Enterprise Application Integration* (Addison-Wesley). He serves as keynote speaker at many leading technology conferences on cloud computing, SOA, enterprise application integration, and enterprise architecture, and has appeared on a number of television and radio shows as a computing expert. His latest book is *Cloud Computing and SOA Convergence in Your Enterprise, a Step-by-Step Approach.*"

What is an Enterprise Service Bus (ESB)?

An enterprise service bus (ESB) is a type of software used for designing and implementing the interaction and communication between applications in real time. Its primary use is in enterprise application integration (EAI) of heterogeneous and complex architectures.

What are the Capabilities that an ESB Needs to Provide for Data Integration?

ESBs provide the ability to consume data from source data storage, process that data in flight, such as transformation and semantic mediations, and then place the data in the target data storage. While not typically suited for ETL-type operations, the ESB provides event-driven data integration that may occur in and between several heterogeneous systems and databases. This is an evolution of the message brokers, created in the 1990s, which provide similar features.

What kind of metadata does an ESB require/keep regarding data movement and transformation?

It largely depends on the ESB, but typically they store:

- Data structure
- Data semantics
- Data constraints
- Data service information
- Data ownership

- Data security information
- Data governance information

What is Involved in an ESB Configuration (What has to be done, What Kind of Resources (Skills) are Required)?
Again, it depends on the ESB. However, general activities should include:

- Understanding the source, and the target systems, including data semantics, data structure, and mechanisms for connectivity.
- Designing the flows between source and target systems.
- Designing the transformations of the data as it flows from source to target.
- Defining service governance and other controls that should be placed on the data at rest and in flight.
- Testing the integration to determine the system's ability to meet the requirements.

What is the Effort (Activities, Resources, Skills) Needed to Operate an ESB in Production?
You need somebody who understands all sources and targets, all flows, all connections and adapters, the ESB software, and how to deal with errors and exceptions.

Have you Had Experiences in Which the ESB Operation was Neglected (Underresourced)?
Most of the failures I've seen don't really involve lack of planning and architecture. Rather, failure occurs when an attempt is made to leverage an ESB inappropriately, perhaps because the vendors have been promoting the product as "SOA in a box". Thus, when the vendors get the technology implemented, they seek to use it as a services broker. ESBs are more about information integration, while typically dealing with services as mechanisms to push and pull data off of the ESB; that does not make it an SOA.

Is Data Integration different for Structured and Unstructured Data? Does an ESB Operation Work for Structured and Unstructured Data? Are there Different Tools?
In order for ESB to work with unstructured data, the data must be placed into some kind of structure that the ESB can handle. However, a few tools are beginning to support unstructured data as a native format as big data becomes more of a driving force. I suspect that most ESBs will morph around the ability to process unstructured data moving forward.

How do you Think ESB Tools are Changing? In What Direction do you Think this Area is Headed?
As mentioned above, ESB tools are morphing around the integration requirements of big data systems, including the ability to deal with both structured and unstructured data, as well as large volumes of data and higher transfer rates. Of course, the interest in cloud computing means that more of them will be localized for more popular public and private clouds, as well as some ESBs provided as a service out of a cloud.

Service-oriented architecture (SOA)

Service-oriented architecture is a design principle in which software is designed and built in pieces that provide well-defined services when requested. The services may involve performing some activity or returning some information or answer. Most current custom software development is designed and programmed using SOA. Vendor packages that can be purchased usually also provide the capability to interact as services that can be invoked through an API . Service-oriented architecture is particularly relevant in integration because the well-defined nature of the services directs the various systems and technologies on the protocol for interactions. SOA best practice principles include a loose coupling of services, such that the particular technology used in implementations of the various services should not be of interest to users or applications trying to invoke those services, but simply the result. Data services in SOA are those that either provide or update information.

The differences between an ESB and an SOA are first that an ESB is a tool or engine whereas SOA is a design philosophy, and second, that ESB is usually used in a heterogeneous application environment of differing technologies that want to pass data around, whereas SOA implies a more heterogeneous technology environment. An ESB might be connecting some applications that have been written as services, but usually includes applications that have not been written consistently and so the ESB provides the needed layers of technical translation and transformation. If all applications that need to interact have been developed using consistent standards and protocols, then an ESB might be unnecessary, but it still provides the orchestration necessary for the interactions. In the real world of integrating new applications with older legacy applications, an ESB is needed. Coding the overhead of orchestration of the interactions of the application into the code of the application software would be a great burden that is easier to offload onto the specialized ESB technology, just as we offload the overhead of data storage to a database management system.

A bit of tension exists between efficient real-time data integration solutions and pure service-oriented architecture. Software designers and application architects may want to implement all things in an application as services, in order to stay true to the design principles of SOA. However, in most applications it may be more efficient for the application programmers to understand how the data is actually being accessed, such as through an ESB or a database management system (DBMS), and designed and coded according to the efficiencies of the underlying data solutions. This issue can be contentious. Much of the functionality of the service layer, or code, around a data service, such as security access checking, may be redundant, duplicating the services performed by the underlying database management software. Solutions coded to retrieve or update data that don't take into account the underlying solution may be so slow as to be unworkable, with unacceptable delay in response, or latency.

Improvements in solutions and technologies have started to make the need to understand the underlying implementation of data services somewhat less necessary. See the discussion of data virtualization in Chapter 20 later in this book. Achieving balance of data integration solutions and SOA working together depends on finding the right balance in granularity when defining services. For operational efficiency, it is not a good idea to define data services of too fine granularity; it is better to define application services that perform recognizable business functions. Again, this may contrast with some SOA design principles, but in practice it may be necessary to loosen some pure theory in order to achieve better performance efficiency.

Service-oriented architectures include a registry of available services and how they are invoked. Although originally the protocol used with SOA was SOAP (simple object access protocol), it has become common to use alternative protocols such as REST (REpresentational State Transfer).

Extensible markup language (XML)

The more removed things are that need to interact, such as organizations, applications, or services, the more necessary it is that the interaction method is flexible and well defined. Most service interactions are defined to use XML (extensible markup language) as the data interchange format to pass information. Use of XML is not a requirement, and there are some performance inefficiencies involved in parsing XML, but XML has been the de facto standard for message interactions for the last decade. It is a useful approach to defining interactions because it is readable by both humans and machines and each piece of data or content being passed includes a description of what that data is, as a "markup" or "tag." Therefore, all data in the XML format is accompanied by at least a brief explanation of what the data means. Data interchanges using XML don't have to have a predetermined agreement in regard to the format of the data since this metadata can accompany the data contents. Since it is a textural data format, it is very useful for managing documents as well as messages and interactions. Other self-documenting data interchange formats that are popular include JSON (Java Script Object Notation).

Just because an interface is said to be in XML does not indicate more than a basic technology choice. It certainly does not indicate what type of data can be found in the XML. It is like saying that software is written using a certain programming language. In fact, there are many languages based on XML syntax.

XML may be presented in a predefined format, following a DTD (document type definition), or it may contain information in an unexpected format but following the rules of a "well-formed" XML document. Interactions with an SOA service would need to follow an expected format or schema as defined by the service.

INTERVIEW WITH AN EXPERT: M. DAVID ALLEN ON XML AND DATA INTEGRATION

Following is an interview with M. David Allen on the importance and use of XML in data integration.

M. David Allen has been working on data integration for about 13 years, focused mostly on the use of XML. He is co-author of *XML in Data Management* published by Morgan Kaufmann and has written a number of articles on aspects of XML schema development and the use of XML messaging formats in data interoperability solutions.

What is XML?

XML is a markup language. It is a set of rules that specify how to encode data in a way that is easily readable by software. XML is not just one format for data, but it contains ways of building as many different formats as a user might need. Most of the time, when people refer to XML they are actually talking about a particular vocabulary or data model built using XML technologies, but XML itself is extremely general and flexible. What is common to all applications of XML is that they all use elements, attributes, and content to create documents.

How is XML Used in Data Integration?

When asking about how XML is related to data integration and how it is used, we need to look at the big picture of XML, which can refer to many different families of technologies. They are all used across the gamut of data integration. XML databases store instance documents; extraction tools pull data out of non-XML databases and format them as XML messages; enterprise service buses can inspect XML messages and route them based on their contents; XML describes the bits and bytes of what often crosses the wire in an integration; software written in XML (i.e., XSLT) can change the form of the data as it moves; and other tools provide native interfaces between XML documents and legacy software. While most integration challenges won't use XML everywhere, XML solutions are present and in use for just about every sub-niche of data integration.

Why is XML Particularly Useful for Data Integration?

XML is useful because it is well-suited to both structured and unstructured information (flexible). XML also represents an open standard that helps prevent lock-in to any particular proprietary technology. That was one of its original strengths when it came out, and while that advantage is no longer unique, it is still valuable. It integrates well with many other widely adopted lower-level technical standards (URIs, URLs, Unicode). XML has a very mature technology and tool base, and it has a wide variety of technical practitioners in the job market who are familiar with it. It came along at a time when computing was just breaking away from proprietary standards, and this "early mover" advantage means that many tools which don't even process XML will at least have some functionality to export their data as XML.

Have you Seen any Data Integration Projects Where XML Issues Led to Significant Problems? Or Where Insufficient Focus was put on XML Issues?

Yes. Often the problems with XML stem from naïve mappings to and from XML. Simply put, XML is a document-oriented, hierarchical data format. What people are moving in and out of XML though typically isn't, and the mapping may be problematic. For example, I've seen projects attempt to replicate a relational model inside of XML, resulting in XML schema layouts that were much too large to be feasible. I've also seen projects miss the point of the structure that XML can offer, ending up packing complex text records inside of a single element attribute, that later needed to be parsed out with specialized software. Just like anything else that requires a data model, there are many pitfalls possible surrounding efforts made in the modeling stage.

Have you Had Experiences Where Particular Attention was paid to the XML for Data Integration?

Generally, XML does not get the attention; most of the attention goes to the business need, the budgeting realities, and the technical choices that have to be made to minimize the impact on legacy systems. XML, then, is just one of many technical approaches used to create a business effect in a much larger context. Some might even argue that the best integration solutions are those that work so well that users do not even need to know or care whether XML was involved.

Even within technical teams, XML only infrequently gets the attention. Technical teams are often composed of those who really understand the underlying systems (whether they are oracle databases, document repositories, or whatever else) or who really understand the available tools (ETL, mapping, and so on). Much of the time, they'll have background knowledge of XML, but the focus will be not on the XML, but on the underlying data store, the tool, or the design approach.

What Kinds of Tools or Technologies are Used to Support Data Integration and XML?

A host of data-mapping tools are available which generally focus on describing correspondences between one model and another, and on generating transform code. There are a great number of modeling tools that permit the creation of high-level models in language like UML, which can be "forward engineered" into XML models. Many ETL tools will have options for extracting or transforming data through XML.

Some databases store nothing but XML documents (MarkLogic, eXist, Sedna). These are often used as native stores in the case of unstructured information integration, and they may be used as a staging area, or as part of a processing pipeline for a larger application that needs to work with XML.

At lower layers of application development, there are absolutely critical tools that perform Object/XML mapping (XML Beans, JAXB), permitting developers to serialize and de-serialize XML documents into a series of in-memory objects in Java or C#. This class of tools also includes database to XML mapping packages, which can expose the contents of a relational database directly as XML documents.

One way to summarize this information would be as follows: XML is so ubiquitous that for just about any other technology (programming language, relational database, modeling language, etc.) there is a tool available that specializes in mapping from that technology to XML documents and back again. All of them are used to support data integration efforts in different niches.

How is Data Integration XML for Structured Data Different From Data Integration XML for Unstructured Data? Is the Data Integration Different?

The integration approaches are very different. Integration of highly structured data can often take advantage of approaches that exploit the details of the data model. Unstructured data by its nature usually doesn't have as much of (or any) formal model describing its contents, which calls for a different set of techniques for integration, and also certain limitations on the uses you can expect to get out of the data.

How do you Think the Area of XML and Data Integration is Changing? Where do you Think this Area is Headed?

The area is changing quite a bit. Several kinds of changes affect XML and data integration, which I'd like to discuss individually.

- Overall integration architecture (EAI and EII versus SOAP versus RESTful architecture)
- How to manage the heterogeneity of formats and models: Should we have one standard?
- How applications are developed (software development methodology)
- How data is processed and stored (big data, map/reduce, etc.)

When XML was first created, the focus of integration architecture appeared to be on heavyweight EAI and EII approaches. As time passed and service-oriented architecture began to get the lion's share of attention, large stacks of XML technologies (the Web services architecture stack) were developed to support that approach, including Simple Object Access Protocol (SOAP), Web Services Description Language (WSDL), Universal Description Discovery and Integration (UDDI), and so on. Today mainstream development focuses on RESTful architecture (Representational State Transfer) at least as much (if not more) than SOA. The design approach behind RESTful services has built into it the notion that resources may have multiple representations—in JSON, XML, and other formats as well. So in roughly 15 years of XML, we've gone through three major architecture shifts, and I wouldn't put my money on RESTful architecture being the last one!

A good amount of data integration work has focused on trying to get data into one single XML format that everyone would agree upon. The spoke-and-hub diagram is often shown to describe the benefit of this approach; instead of having many data formats and an order of n-squared translation problem, the spoke-and-hub design with a single XML format requires only n translations, which is the best possible case. While a single message format is optimal, in many cases it may not be practical, either because all of the stakeholders cannot agree on any one format, or because their uses for the data differ too much. One change I think we're seeing now is a move toward a more pragmatic compromise. Indeed, if there are 15 different formats, the translation burden is too high. But the name of the game is not necessarily to eliminate all of this heterogeneity, but to get it down to a manageable amount. Many modern RESTful services support both XML and JSON, and sometimes a third format. Supporting 3 formats isn't ideal, but it is much better than supporting 10, and may be much easier than getting an entire community of users and developers with very different needs to agree on just one.

So what's changing? Using more than one approach for integration at the same time seems to be gaining acceptance as a good engineering practice to balance trade-offs. In the past, it was often seen as a failure to implement a proper hub-and-spoke approach. In my view, this is a very good development and a move towars pragmatic design, since the number of systems and the complexity of integration problems are only increasing with time.

Another thing that's changing a lot is the application development ecosystem. There's much more focus on agile development methodologies and their offshoots, as well as on big data and nontraditional data stores that aren't relational under the covers. Changes to application development methodologies matter a great deal for data integration work because they impact not only how the applications we're trying to integrate are built, but how the integration solutions themselves are built. Two of the key correct assumptions behind these new approaches are that you cannot know all of the requirements ahead of time and that systems should be flexible enough to permit constant change and adaptation.

Big data databases are focusing on different data structures such as direct graphs, JSON documents, and key/value stores. New processing methods such as map/reduce have come along with big data approaches. This all constitutes a lot of change for data integration, because creating the big data stores in themselves is often an integration exercise, and because today's NoSQL database is tomorrow's data integration headache!

When Would the Use of JSON be More Appropriate or Preferred to XML?

JSON's strengths shine when the data sent needs to change rapidly, or when the data format needs to support Web application developments that have a heavy javascript component. Because JSON is generally schema-less, it works very well for rapid prototyping, when the format of the message may change several times per week as an application begins to take shape. This is in contrast to most XML approaches, which would require maintenance of the XML schema, and possibly other software artifacts as well. Many Web applications nowadays will opt to make their data available as JSON because they expect that user applications written in a mixture of HTML5, CSS, and JavaScript will need to take advantage of the data, and JSON is the friendliest possible format for javascript programmers.

Data replication and change data capture

The original purpose of data replication was to enable two data stores to be kept in synch with one another, with a minimal amount of information required to be passed between them as well as a minimal amount of impact on the source application. Data replication was used frequently because of the tremendous latency, or time delay, involved in data being accessed or updated across long distances. If an organization had a data set that they wanted to use around the world, for example, it was more efficient to keep multiple copies of the data close to each of the places where it needed to be updated or used and then keep the data synchronized using data replication. The downside was having the multiple copies and having to pay for the disk storage each required.

Data replication, or change data capture, is usually a capability offered by a database management system or other data storage solution. Rather than send copies of the data structures changed between instances of the replicated data, data replication usually sends copies of the data structure change *log entries*. Since log entries are usually very small compared to the entire data structure, sending log entries is smaller and faster. Also, data replication minimizes the impact on the applications: The monitoring of changes is done on the log and not on the data used by the application.

Change data capture (see Figure 13.2) is a very effective way of allowing data to be used across remote locations; it was very necessary at a time when wide area network access was very, very slow. Now, emerging technologies are finding this to be an effective way of solving many other latency and impact issues. Because the source data structure itself is not accessed, the impact on the source system is minimal and it is useful in cases where the response time of the source system can't be affected.

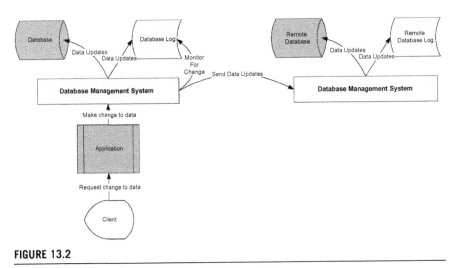

FIGURE 13.2

Change Data Capture.

Enterprise application integration (EAI)

Enterprise application integration (EAI) is a type of data integration architecture or approach. Its subject covers all the techniques of integrating applications of various technologies, including the hub and spoke approach, using ESBs, and various interaction patterns such as publish and subscribe. The point of enterprise application integration is to connect applications in the portfolio that were developed and implemented at differing times and using differing technologies, thus integrating heterogeneous applications.

The best practice in data integration is to interact through the applications and let the application code handle access to the underlying data structures. Even if an application does not have a predefined set of services or APIs, it is still best to try to build a wrapper that invokes the application code to access the data or data function needed. Many vendor packages are quite insistent that interfaces should not bypass the application code, and it is best not to, especially for any update to the data stores underlying an application.

Enterprise information integration (EII)

In the unfortunate event that the application code to access the needed data cannot be invoked but must be bypassed, then it may be necessary to access the application data structures directly.

A data integration interface directly to the data structures underlying a legacy application bypasses the application code because the code needed to access the data structures is not accessible. As shown in Figure 13.3, a small amount of code

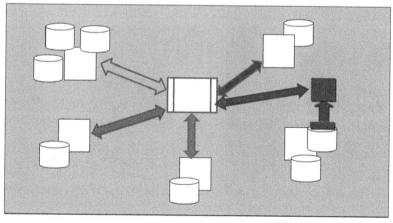

FIGURE 13.3

Accessing a Data Structure Directly in Enterprise Information Integration.

needs to be written to bypass the application and access the data directly. The data integration code to access the legacy data structures would be written using the standard application development tools, the standard data integration tools, the legacy data structure tools, or an appropriate combination. For example, if the application where customer data is produced is a legacy system with an underlying relational database and the application doesn't have an API or service defined, code may be written in the database (bypassing the application). This code will monitor for any updates and indicate that the customer information that was updated be written onto the outgoing queue for the adapter running on that server and be published to interested applications by the enterprise service bus.

Data Integration Modeling

14

INFORMATION IN THIS CHAPTER

Canonical modeling

Creating a hub and spoke model for real-time system interoperability has significant benefits, as it allows for an additional system to be placed in the portfolio and integrated with the other systems simply by establishing interfaces from the new system to only one other system: the "hub" or central system that interfaces with all others. Using a hub and spoke architecture can significantly reduce the complexity of the system interactions and interfaces that must be maintained from an exponential number of interfaces to a linear number of interfaces. The additional investment needed to use a hub and spoke approach, however, is the creation of one additional (possibly only virtual) system: The "hub" must be added to the portfolio. The "hub" application of the portfolio will usually be part of an enterprise service bus or a middleware component of a vendor package that provides the required functionality. The hard part for an organization is not just implementing the technology but defining a data model for the hub that can sufficiently handle all the passing of data necessary between the applications: a canonical model for the shared data of the organization. The canonical model for the organization is not necessarily all the data of the organization, but all the data that needs to be shared.

The word "canon" means a rule, but it has come to be used to mean, as in this case, the unique distinguishing standard of something. A "canonical data model" for an organization can mean the documentation of the important business terms and items in that organization with definitions of each business term and the relationships between the terms. In regards to data integration, it also means

99

defining the data in the central hub of interoperability, which can be used for the pass-through of all real-time interfaces in the organization. Data in the hub is not persistent: The hub is virtual and refers to data that is in the process of being translated to or from the format of one of the applications in the portfolio. So, although there may be no data stored in the hub, the data model of the hub may be extensive since it must incorporate all the data in the organization that is to be shared between systems. The goal of this model is to provide a set of reusable common objects at an enterprise or business-domain level to enhance system interoperability.

INTERVIEW WITH AN EXPERT: DAGNA GAYTHORPE ON CANONICAL MODELING AND DATA INTEGRATION

Dagna Gaythorpe has been involved in data modeling, architecture, and management for 20 years. She has performed the technical proofreading of two books: *Data Modelling Essentials*, by Graeme Simsion and Graham Witt, published by Elsevier in 2005; and *Data Model Patterns—Metadata* by David Hay, published by Elsevier in 2006. She is a regular attendee and speaker at conferences in the United States and Europe, and is on the boards of DAMA International and DAMA UK.

What is Canonical Modeling?

Canonical modeling is the basis of a spoke and hub approach to data mapping. There are other approaches; the main one is point to point, which is far more time consuming. The canonical approach uses a common central model and maps everything to that, so that (assuming the mapping has been done correctly) it is possible to say with certainty that field A in this system holds the same data as field B in that one (although they have different names and formats). This speeds up the data-mapping approach, as each field only has to be mapped once, to the canonical model. After the first data set is mapped, the point to point mappings for each pair of systems become part of the canonical metadata set, centered on the common canonical data item.

If bespoke systems are being developed (so the database is being designed for the purpose), then using the canonical model for the database design means that no transformation of the data coming in or going out is needed. In my view, use of the canonical model as the basis for all bespoke database design is an excellent strategic approach. Over time it will reduce the amount of transformation that needs to be done, as well as lessen the "what does this system mean by X?" sort of confusion that makes life "interesting" for business and management information reporting.

How is Data Integration (i.e., Moving and Transforming Data) Related to Canonical Modeling?

If the data being transferred is in a common format, then it only needs to be transformed to or from that common format on its way out of, or into, each database. So instead of a transformation routine for every source, the targets only need one routine, from the canonical format—unless the target used the canonical data model for the database design, in which case they don't need to transform, just load. And each system (that doesn't use the canonical forms) does need to transform its data on the way out.

For most organizations, the move to a canonical approach may take years and will happen as old applications are replaced or as a side-effect of other work. Thus, in reality most systems will be doing some point-to-point transformations alongside the canonical common ones. This is why I mentioned that it should be a strategic approach: It will take a lot of time (unless there is some big-bang transformation going on), but it will deliver more and more benefits as that time passes and more systems "come into the fold."

What Kind of Metadata is Kept Regarding Canonical Modeling and Data Integration?

In addition to the metadata specifying the canonical model and the mappings from the source systems to target systems, I would also keep the cross references, recording where each item (entity or attribute) in the canonical model appears in all the other mapped systems; identifying the systems where it gets created (bonus points if there is only 1); and for major entities holding some sort of life cycle, showing how it moves through the systems and what they do to it and what they use it for, including where it gets sent outside the organization, if it does.

At What Point in a Data Integration Project is a Canonical Model Created? Why? What Activities are Involved in Developing a Canonical Model?

Creation of a canonical model begins as soon as you start looking at sources and targets. Ideally, you start with the enterprise data model, if there is one. If there isn't, then the canonical data model can be the start of the enterprise model. If there is an enterprise model, or a suitable logical model, then I start by mapping one system to that. This is almost always in a spread sheet—which makes sorting and reviewing easier. If there is no suitable model, then I have to build one, and map the other systems to it. If there is no existing model, but an obvious core system exists, use that as the starting point.

How is Canonical Modeling Similar to or Different From Other Kinds of Modeling? Is it Necessary to Create a Logical and Physical Version of a Canonical Model? Other Versions?

Canonical modeling has a lot in common with enterprise and programming modeling. In all of them, the model is describing the common vocabulary of the part of the enterprise being modeled, and that vocabulary will be used by other people as the basis for what they do. It is also likely that few, if any, of the "consumers" of these models will use the whole thing. They are likely to use a subset of it, possibly most of it, but that few if any systems, programs, or other developments will likely use the whole model. The main exceptions to this are ERP systems and data warehouses (so if there is an ERP system or warehouse connected to the area the canonical model is covering, that is a good place to start looking for or developing the canonical model).

In general, I am in favor of keeping the modeling as simple as possible. This includes minimizing the number of models. In my opinion, rarely does any one thing need more than two models—one higher level (e.g., logical) and one detailed (e.g., physical). In the case of canonical modeling, I favor a single model. It will probably start out logical, and gradually get more physical as time passes and more of the rules and definitions are recorded. This happens because the canonical model isn't actually a model: It is (if it is working) a repository/dictionary where things get translated and identified.

Have you Seen any Data Integration Projects Where Canonical Modeling Issues Led to Significant Problems?

I have encountered instances where a large project ran into trouble because the various groups working on it saw the canonical model as an academic exercise that was getting in their way. As a result, they put a lot of effort into developing point-to-point interfaces, and worked in their own silos, developing their own models, which was a huge waste of effort.

Have you Had Experiences Where Particular Attention was Paid to Canonical Modeling for Data Integration? How did that Work? What Was the Impact on the Project Schedule?

Two instances come to mind. One was a data warehouse project involving taking and merging data from a number (more than 10) of systems that all had the same basic function, but all handled it differently (even the two copies of the same package that had been implemented). They had to merge the data and then pass a coherent version on to another set of systems. In the second instance, the developers decided that they were implementing SOA not as a program, but as the way they would do things in the future. In both cases, the canonical model was used as the basis for all the data transfers, ETL, and messaging—not as a "this is how you must do it" approach, but as a "this is how we do it and if you want to do it any other way, please justify the extra work and time you will take" approach. The canonical model was used as a way of getting things done much faster than a piecemeal approach would have allowed.

Have you Had Experiences Where Canonical Modeling was Neglected on a Data Integration Project? What Happened? What was the Impact on the Project schedule?

I tend to sneak a canonical model into a data integration project as a matter of course. I describe it as the standard layout, and people tend to accept it.

Is it Generally Accepted on Real-Time Data Integration Projects that a Canonical Model is Needed? Why or Why Not?

I myself accept it, but I have encountered resistance from time to time, mostly from people who want everyone else to do things the way their piece of the world does. Further, they think that it is perfectly reasonable to expect everyone else to make the extra effort to accommodate them. This is never a happy situation and can lead to annoyance among the people who are expected to make the accommodation.

What Kinds of Tools or Technologies are Used to Support Canonical Modeling? Do you think the Technologies for Canonical Modeling, Especially Around Data Integration, are Changing?

Modeling tools are getting more sophisticated now and are integrating with each other more than they did formerly. But there are still problems getting process and data models linked, for example, and if an organization has more than one data-modeling tool, then canonical modeling can become challenging, since those tools often don't talk to each other. This is one of the reasons that spreadsheets still seem to be the main tool and type of repository, along with the ease of adding things to a spreadsheet. The term '*canonical model* seems to cover a whole range of ideas, from the messages used to exchange data to the core data being exchanged The notation used varies widely, depending on what the people developing the model are comfortable with. I think that as the idea of canonical modeling develops, and as it settles down and matures, we will see it incorporated into data- and process-modeling tools.

Are the Tools for Canonical Modeling Different for Structured and Unstructured Data?

They are different in the same way that the tools for modeling structured and unstructured data are different—though I think it has more to do with the notations and methods used than with the tools used to do them.

How do you Think the Area of Canonical Modeling is Changing? Where do you Think this Area is Headed?

I think that canonical modeling will eventually stop being something we have to ask about, and will start to be seen as one of the inputs into data design, in the same way that a logical model is now. And I also think (and hope) that it will be done as part of the enterprise information/data architecture function, and supplied to anyone who needs it, alongside the common logical model, ideally, as part of (and an extension to) that logical model.

Message modeling

Modeling the layouts of the interfaces between systems or organizations is very similar to but slightly different from modeling persistent data in a database. It may save time and effort, depending on the modeler, to model in the language of the interface technology and not just a logical representation. In other words, the goal of the message model is to implement message layouts, not just a logical model. Much time is spent these days transforming persistent data models from object to relational presentations (or vice versa) because of the differences between the programming language and the data structures in relational databases. To avoid this, modeling messages should be done in a format or manner consistent with the target implementation. This usually means using an XML or JSON format or some format consistent with the enterprise service bus (ESB) or SOA technology to be used.

Industry standard models are a very good starting point for an organization's message model because they usually deal with the common business objects for the organization's industry. Extensive numbers of industry models are currently available, which have thousands of man-hours in developing and reviewing. Electronic Data Interchange (EDI) is ubiquitous for retail industry interactions between organizations and Society for Worldwide Interbank Financial Telecommunication (SWIFT) for banking and financial securities interactions between financial organizations. Most industries have standard industry models. These industry models may only handle the types of transactions that would take place between financial organizations and may have to be extended for interactions necessary between applications within the same organization.

Master Data Management 15

Introduction to master data management

Master data management (MDM) is an architecture that has been developed for managing the subset of data in the organization around important areas such as customer, product, and organizational structure; information that we call master data. These items frequently are the "keys" in the transactional data of the organization; for example, a product is sold to a customer and the revenue or costs are attributed to an employee or a part of the sales organization. It is critically important that the information about master data is correct because mistakes can become greatly magnified when used in transactions. It is also of great importance that all parts of the organization are working off the same version of master data. Customers no longer find it acceptable to have to change their address or other information multiple times with different parts of an organization just because different computer systems happen to store the customer's information in multiple places.

Reasons for a master data management solution

For most organizations, justifying an investment in the creation of a master data hub requires only a simple analysis of the costs associated with previous inconsistencies and mistakes, since master data problems can mushroom into huge issues in the transaction processing systems. We want to place particular focus on the data quality of organization's master data, and we want to have an agreed upon single or consolidated source of master data that can be used by the whole organization. Another straightforward justification for a master data solution is the cost of updating master data in multiple systems.

Data integration is critical to master data management to manage the consolidation of data from multiple operational systems and sources, as well as to distribute the master data to the systems and groups that want to use it. Managing the movement of data to and from the hub of master data is so crucial to the success of MDM system implementations that master data management architects sometimes describe the whole area of data integration as a part within the subject of master data management.

Organizations usually implement MDM solutions for one or both of two reasons: to provide a consolidated view of an organization's master data for reporting purposes, or to provide a central source of master data for transaction purposes. If all an organization is trying to do is consolidate master data together from the transaction processing systems for reporting or for their data warehouse, then the movement of the master data together to the master data hub might very well be implemented using a nightly batching of updates from the transaction systems to the hub using a batch data movement solution. In the case of nightly batch updates of master data, the consolidation of information might only be occurring in the data warehouse, and so there may be no need for a separate master data hub.

For organizations that are attempting to consolidate master data for real-time use by transactional systems, a separate master data hub is usually created by acquiring and implementing a vendor master data software solution. The vendor solutions have a great deal of the functionality needed built in, including sometimes a starting data model and capabilities to link to many standard real-time data movement solutions.

Purchased packages and master data

The challenge of managing master data is getting more difficult. When most application systems in an organization were custom developed, there was usually just one set of master data in the organization that would be used by all the applications. With the advent of purchased vendor applications to perform common functions such as financial consolidation, customer relationship management (CRM), and enterprise resource planning (ERP), each vendor application has its own set of master data structures which have to be kept in synch with the custom master data. Since buying application solutions is considered best practice where possible over building application solutions, the problems of integrating master data are ubiquitous for all organizations. ERP systems sometimes promote themselves by saying that all the functionality is integrated and there is only one set of master data used across all the applications in the ERP. However, many organizations end up implementing multiple ERP applications or multiple instances of one ERP. No organization can get away with implementing no additional systems other than the ERP.

Reference data

Sometimes reference data is differentiated from master data. Reference data usually refers to the standard sets of values that certain fields might be able to contain, such as countries or other geographical options, statuses, or types. Frequently, the source of definitive references data is external to the organization. Providing one source of a particular type of reference data in an organization can help avoid a lot of duplicate effort and prevent inconsistent results and reporting. Differentiating reference data from other types of master data can become very confusing. Certain aspects of an organization's product data, for example, may be sourced from an external organization and may be called either reference data or product data. Both master data and reference data are used as key attributes in operational transactional data and financial data. Although reference data is usually less changeable or dynamic than master data, certain forms of reference data are dynamic and so require constant updating.

Uusually there is little to be gained in maintaining a strict separation between master data and reference data. As with master data, each type of reference data should have a person or group responsible for overseeing the management, update and use of that data in the organization.

Masters and slaves

The architecture of a master data management solution is very similar to the hub and spoke architecture used for managing the complexity of data interfaces. The difference between the two is that a master data hub is instantiated, not just logical, whereas a data integration hub is simply a logical concept. Also, business users may be aware of a master data hub, but may not be aware of the data integration communication "hub" in a hub and spoke architecture because in effect all that happens is that the data gets transformed into a common intermediate model or canonical model.

Figure 15.1 shows some applications, all of which are maintaining the same kind of master data, such as product data, and need to share any updates between them, plus the other reporting and transactional systems that need a consolidated view of the master data. This kind of peer-to-peer sharing of updates is very

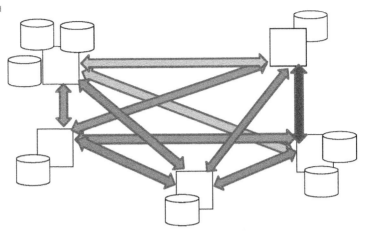

FIGURE 15.1

Integration Without a Master Involves an Exponential Number of Interactions.

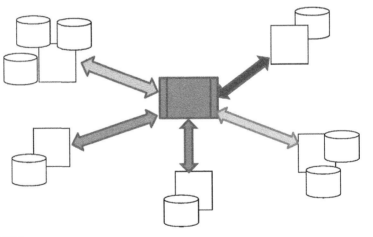

FIGURE 15.2

Master Data Application Interaction Only Requires a Linear Number of Interactions.

difficult and complex to control, as well as having an exponential number of interfaces to manage.

Figure 15.2 shows the configuration of applications where the master has been identified for the particular data domain. Updates are only made in the master or are all passed to the master, which then provides a consolidated view of that master data domain to all applications that require it and have appropriate access. The master data application may be different for each data domain, since the appropriate master for product data, for example, may be different than customer data. Similarly, the applications that are getting master data updates may be different for each domain.

The architecture for master data management does not necessarily require an additional application to be implemented that will play the part of the master for a domain of data, such as customer, product, or employee. The critical first step may be to determine that an existing operational system holds the de facto master of data for that domain, or the "system of record." All other places where the master data resides are designated as the "slaves," and the ability to make updates to the master data is disabled on the slave systems. The financial consolidation and reporting application, for example, is usually considered to be the master for clients who are billed, since it is necessary to report consolidated financials and profitability by client. Depending on the business and application architecture, many of the core master data domains may be effectively mastered in the organization's central enterprise resource planning (ERP) system.

In practice, however, assigning the role of master to an existing operational or financial system is usually less than optimal. Financial systems are generally focused on updates at the end of the financial period, such as monthly, quarterly, or yearly, and the responsible system users are not concerned with making sure the master data is updated in real time. Operational systems and ERPs focus on customers ordering goods and services, and while they may make a very good source for a master data hub, they usually have behavior and actual content that makes playing the role of the master data application difficult. Frequently, not all customers or all products are located in a single operational system, and adding more items just for the sake of master data management is inconvenient for the central users of the system. In addition, maintaining that data is not a high priority. Adding more information, functionality, or fields to either ERPs or custom operational systems for the sake of master data management is usually a very low priority, if even acceptable, to the central users and support groups around production operational systems. For most organizations and for most types of master data, the volume of master data is not a struggle to manage, especially in comparison to transactional and event information. However, we usually want to maintain a full history of all the changes with master data, especially for auditing and customer service, and operational systems only want to maintain current information for use in transaction processing. In practice, therefore, it has been found that creating a separate application in the existing application portfolio as the master data hub is a best practice.

Sometimes a separate master data application covers each data domain. Sometimes one application is created that supports multiple domains. Having one cross-domain application seems to make the most sense initially, since this system will have to possess many of the same interfaces for each of the mastered domains, such as to the enterprise data warehouse. However, if different business groups are the owners of the different domains of master data, they may find it more convenient to have separate applications that can be managed and controlled independently by the business groups that are the central users and managers. A federated solution by domain may provide more agility to the separate business and application support teams, but will be more costly to operate because there are separate support teams and little shared code.

Organizations usually start by implementing one key master data domain that is particularly critical to their business and that justifies an investment in a master data solution. Some organizations start with the customer domain or some aspect of it, whereas other organizations find the product domain to be a natural starting place. Many organizations find that starting by mastering their reference data provides a great deal of return and allows them to start or pilot in a "small" area.

External data

In many cases, some or all of the master data in a particular domain is acquired from a source external to the organization, either free from a government or standard site or purchased. The organization needs to provide a location where the external data is instantiated, reviewed, cleansed or reformatted, and made available to the entire organization. In certain businesses, external master data is so critical that large organizations sometimes find they are purchasing the same data multiple times for different business functions. Financial securities definitions and prices are critical to businesses dealing with financial market data. Drug information is critical to life sciences businesses. These are just a few examples of the types of data acquired from external sources.

Master data management functionality

A key functionality that master data solutions need to provide is the capability to identify when the same piece of master data is coming from multiple sources, or multiple times from the same source. Among the potential duplicates it is determined, either automatically or manually, which one is the correct and most recent version. The matching code can be very complex using "fuzzy logic" and identifying different spellings or misspellings of names and addresses. The cross reference of identifiers from the various source and transaction systems that refer to the same piece of master data is maintained for reporting consolidation and future updates. Sometimes the master data hub is configured to send the best version or any updates of the master data back to all the source and transaction systems that need it, as well as to the reporting systems and data warehouse. If operational up-to-date master data needs to be provided, it is necessary to have real-time data transfer between the master data hub solution and the sources and transactions systems that provide the operational master data.

Although adding another application to the organization's portfolio and frequently being very expensive, vendor solutions usually provide tremendous benefits to an organization's ability to quickly implement a master data management solution: They provide the matching and de-duplication code; integrate easily with most standard real-time data integration solutions or easily provide a solution; provide a cross reference of identifiers used for the master data across the organization; and even sometimes provide a potential canonical model for important master data. Justifying the expense of purchasing an MDM solution is usually quite easy to do.

Obviously, a master data hub is a data hub. Therefore, if an organization does not already have a hub and spoke solution implemented for other data integration reasons, it may not necessarily choose to do so just to implement the master data hub but rather just implement real time, point to point integration for master data. The master data solution plays the part of the hub (in hub and spoke architecture) for the subset of data in the organization that is master data, thus simplifying the potential complexity of application interfaces.

Types of master data management solutions—registry and data hub

There are two flavors of master data management solutions in addition to whether the solution is only for reporting or for use by operational systems. One flavor is to provide a registry of master data information, or a cross reference of where the master data is located and the various identifiers that refer to the same piece of master data. Although a registry solution may still identify multiple places within and across applications where the same piece of master data has been assigned multiple references or identifiers, the registry doesn't necessarily store all the master data but rather just a pointer to where the master data is located.

The second flavor is to provide a data store where all the master data is copied and maintained. The master data hub doesn't just provide a cross reference to the sources of master data but also supplies a copy of the data and is itself the system of record for the master data. This type of master data hub is also said to provide the "golden copy" or definitive best version of the data for the organization. A primary difference is that with a central hub of master data, changes and corrections to the master data are probably done to the data in the hub and are automatically fed back to other systems. In contrast, changes to master data in the registry model need to be made in the source systems where the master data actually resides.

Data Warehousing with Real-Time Updates

16

INFORMATION IN THIS CHAPTER

Corporate information factory

Bill Inmon defines a data warehouse as "a subject-oriented, integrated, time-variant, nonvolatile collection of data in support of management's decision-making process" (Inmon, 1992). Data warehouses are usually populated periodically (daily, weekly, or monthly) with updates and snapshots from the master data and transaction processing applications in the organization. Figure 16.1 depicts the architecture of a data warehouse and business intelligence solution that receives batch updates periodically.

Operational data store

More current data may be needed for some operational reporting. To meet the need for real-time or near real-time data, an additional data structure may be added to the "corporate information factory" (Inmon, *The Corporate Information Factory*, 1994) or data warehouse architecture: an operational data store (ODS) that integrates real-time updates with master and transactional data for use by operational reports. Since data movement into and out of a data warehouse is usually done in a batch mode, in order to populate the ODS and provide real-time data for reports, the architecture for the corporate information factory needs a real-time data movement capability. Usually, another real-time data movement capability is added, or an existing real-time data movement capability is

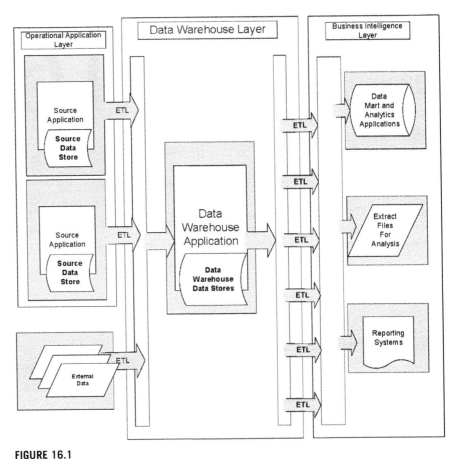

FIGURE 16.1

Corporate Information Factory Architecture.

leveraged. Unfortunately, the batch ETL metadata and transformation logic that already exists for the data warehouse cannot usually be leveraged for the real-time data movement metadata need, so the transformation has to be written for the real-time data movement. Figure 16.1 depicts the architecture of a corporate information factory including the addition of an operational data store (ODS).

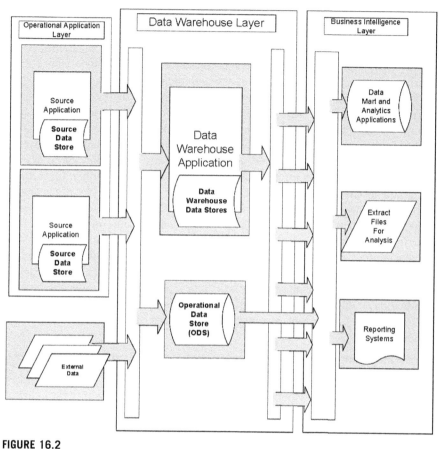

FIGURE 16.2

Corporate Information Factory with ODS.

In some data warehouse architectures, the operational data store is fed from the operational system's real time, and then updates to the data warehouse structure are made on a periodic basis from the ODS. More frequently, however, the batch updates to the data warehouse predate the creation of the ODS, and so it is easier to add the ODS as another structure but not as a replacement as the source of data to the data warehouse. Additionally, one problem with data warehouse implementations is that projects tend to take so long to add more data sources to the data warehouse and then to reports from the data warehouse. Adding another step to the process of getting new data into reports, by making it necessary to also add any additional sources into the ODS would just exacerbate that issue.

Master data moving to the data warehouse

Master data in the data warehouse environment is usually maintained with updates from the operational systems or master data environment rather than snapshots of the entire set of data for each periodic update of the warehouse. If a real-time update capability is added to the warehouse in support of maintaining information in the ODS, then it is also possible and preferable to use that same capability to maintain the master data in the warehouse real time. Changing master data in the data warehouse on a different schedule than the transactional data could change the results viewed in certain reports, depending on how the reports are defined. The master data is usually used in reporting for sorting and grouping the transactional data and is what is called the "dimensions" (Kimball) of the data. Reports have to choose whether to group the transactional data based on the state of the master data at the time of the transaction or at the time the report is written. Different choices may be appropriate for different reports. For example, for a report of sales, if a salesman moves to a different territory, should the report show his historical sales in the new territory or the old? In calculating commissions, a report needs to show his historical sales under him wherever he works in the company, but in showing year over year sales by territory a report needs to show sales under the historical territory.

INTERVIEW WITH AN EXPERT: KRISH KRISHNAN ON REAL-TIME DATA WAREHOUSING UPDATES

Following is a continuation of the interview with Krish Krishnan on the importance and use of data integration in data warehousing. The following discussion is specifically focused on real-time data integration.

Krish Krishnan has spent 12 years designing, architecting, and developing data warehouse solutions, in the last five years focusing on unstructured data integration into the data warehouse. He has been involved in some of the largest and most complex designs and architecture of next-generation data warehouses. He is co-author of *Building the UnStructured Data Warehouse* with Bill Inmon.

When is it Appropriate to Use Real-Time Data Integration with a Data Warehouse? Do you think it is Worthwhile to have both Batch and Real-Time Data Integration Solutions Working with a Data Warehouse?

Real time is a relative term that has been used in the data warehouse industry for a long time. Real-time data integration is useful in financial services, health care, and sensor data management in the current data layers in the data warehouse.

In today's fast-paced data environment, the data processing techniques will involve real-time, micro-batch, and batch processing. We can architect different techniques using these combinations to effectively process data into the data warehouse. Remember that metadata and master data management are key aspects of this mixed-integration architecture.

Are there Special issues Associated with Real-Time Data Integration and Data Warehousing?

To manage real-time data integration in the data warehouse, we need the following architecture layers

- Scalable storage
- Scalable processor and memory architecture
- Fast networks
- Flexible data architecture
- Robust reference data
- Metadata

What are the Considerations for Real-Time Update of Master Data in the Data Warehouse?

Master data management consists of operational, analytical, and "gold copy" layers in the architecture. In order to accommodate the real-time data integration requirements to maintain master data, we need to expand the data processing across the three layers of the master data set. By expanding the operational data architecture, the master data architecture needs to support an object-driven model or an SOA model where the data sets can be self-contained. This approach will provide the best scalable and distributed architecture to manage MDM in real time.

What are the Considerations, Especially Around Data Integration, for Adding an Operational Data Store to a Data Warehouse Configuration?

The ODS or operational data store is an optional layer for data integration in the data warehouse. There are no data model or data type or data architecture changes when comparing an ODS to the source database. In many cases, the ODS is a snapshot of the source databases, and hence there is no specific data integration requirement. However, if the ODS needs to accommodate more than one source database, the data model will need to be modified to accommodate multiple tenants and integrate data in the ODS. Apart from modifying the data model, the physical architecture of the database needs multiple partition and indexing techniques to be implemented for scalability. Data quality is not a prime step in the ODS, but master data and metadata integration is needed to create an auditable environment. In the case of unstructured or big data, I advise that no ODS be created or considered for any form of data processing of this type of data.

Real-Time Data Integration Architecture and Metadata

17

INFORMATION IN THIS CHAPTER

What is real-time data integration metadata?

The metadata associated with real-time data integration is very much the same as for batch data integration. We categorize metadata into three types: business, technical, and operational.

The business metadata for real-time data integration includes the business definitions for the data to be moved and integrated around and between organizations. Security access information, what data can be passed or seen by what applications and users, can be classified under business metadata, although there is a large technical and operational aspect as well.

The technical metadata associated with real-time data integration includes the logical and physical models and layout of the source data, target data, and intermediate canonical model. It also includes the transformations and mappings between the source, target, and intermediate models and physical implementations. The orchestration of behaviors, what data and changes to monitor and what to do when a relevant event occurs, is technical metadata comparable to the batch data interface schedules. The technical metadata provides "lineage" information concerning the exact source for data on a screen, report, or field and how it was transformed.

119

The operational metadata generated from the execution of real-time data integration is very valuable to business users and technical users alike, as well as auditors and regulators. The operational metadata provides "lineage" information about when it was generated or changed. Operational metadata will also provide information on who has changed and accessed data and when.

The technical components and tools that comprise a real time data integration architecture are depicted in Figure 17.1. These are the pieces that are necessary to develop and operate a real time data integration solution.

Modeling

Usually, it is necessary to use a tool to support the development of models needed for real-time data integration, including individual point to point interface models, common interaction or hub model, and data service models. Most tools used for data modeling can be used for real-time data integration modeling as well, although not all have the capability to generate the physical implementation-level models needed, such as XML schemas or data service object classes. It will probably be necessary to reenter the model into the tool being used for the implementation: the ESB, the XML tool or database, and/or the object programming environment. It may be possible to use the implementation tool for initial modeling, but usually modelers like to use some visualization capability while modeling, which is provided by the traditional data-modeling tools and the most frequently used modeling tool: Visio.

In addition to data modeling, the data flows of the interactions are usually modeled using some kind of process modeling tool.

Profiling

As with batch data integration, it is critical to the success of any data integration development project to profile the actual production source and target data prior to the beginning of the project. In this way, it becomes possible to understand whether the potential data involved is of sufficient quality for the purpose intended and whether the appropriate sources and targets have been identified. The same tools and issues associated with batch data integration are appropriate.

Metadata repository

The tools for modeling, profiling, and transforming (the ESB) will have their own metadata repositories, which may be sufficient for managing the relevant

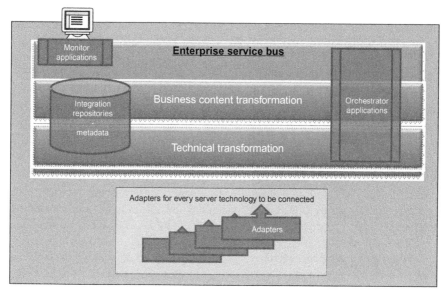

FIGURE 17.1

Real-Time Data Integration Architecture.

metadata for the development and operation of real-time data integration solutions. As with batch data integration metadata, the organization may benefit significantly from a consolidated metadata repository that links the metadata from the various tools and engines and provides an enterprise view and audit trail of the movement and transformation of data around the organization. Of course, a consolidated metadata repository should include the metadata from both batch and real time data integration solutions.

An enterprise metadata repository can become a core capability, providing information to business users on where data in the organization can be found, its relative quality, how it is appropriate to use the data, its history of update, and its access. The ability to provide such an audit trail is also considered best practice, and in many instances, a regulatory requirement.

Enterprise service bus—data transformation and orchestration

The primary tool needed for implementing real-time data integration is an enterprise service bus (ESB), which provides myriad functions necessary for managing the real-time data interfaces in an organization. An ESB provides technical mediation services as well as applying the business semantics information that has been developed. Technically, the ESB provides or integrates with the transport mechanisms of physically moving data between servers, orchestrating the sequence of events and interactions, the interaction and translations needed between different technologies running on the different servers, and monitoring and error recovery. The ESB will integrate with the organization's data security solution as well. The organization will have to specify what data needs to move and when, and then those business decisions can be configured into the ESB.

Technical mediation

In real-time data integration architecture there needs to be software that will handle the technical issues surrounding managing the interactions and messaging. This includes transport for physically moving the data between the servers, which is usually handled by a utility that is installed on all the physical and logical servers involved and included queuing capability for all servers and applications, in order to hold messages until the relevant application is ready to process them. Orchestration capabilities must be present to manage what messages need to be sent to what locations, handling publish and subscribe interactions as well as request and reply. Orchestration includes managing the sequence of events and error processing and recovery.

The technical mediation aspects of the real-time data integration architecture will handle any transformations and interactions necessary for different technologies on different logical and physical servers, including operating systems, file systems, databases, and other data structures. The real-time data integration architecture will need to integrate with the organization's enterprise security solution, to ensure that data is only provided to authorized applications and users.

Business content

The real-time data integration architecture will need a data semantics layer that provides the instructions for mapping the messages between formats recognized by the different applications in the organization and external organizations. This aspect of the architecture is difficult because it requires a good understanding of the business processes and the actual contents of the various data structures of the applications. In order to make real-time data integration work using the hub and spoke architecture approach, it is necessary to have a canonical message model that provides a common format for the data in the organization that needs to be shared between systems or with external organizations. This is an implementation model in the language used by the enterprise service bus, usually something like XML or JSON.

The real-time data integration architecture usually includes a registry of the data services available, so that when adding more applications to the organization portfolio it will be relatively easy to identify what data interfaces have already been defined.

Data movement and middleware

Underlying the tools and engine (ESB) to support real-time data integration are usually some standard utilities and middleware that allow the whole to operate. Of course, there are the various operating systems and database management systems of the applications to be linked on which the data integration tools and engines run. Also, the enterprise service bus as well as most of the SOA applications will require a standard application middleware engine (J2EE).

Within each technical environment being integrated there will have to be a data movement utility that the ESB can use to move data from and to the various servers. Usually the preference would be for one utility that has flavors that run on the various platforms required.

External interaction

Interfaces with external organizations tend to be more loosely coupled than interfaces between applications within an organization. Certainly the systems usually don't require the external party to be operating in order to be able to continue operating, although as in all things there are exceptions. The interfaces with external organizations have to be more fault tolerant since the communications between the organizations may be more difficult. Security must be a high concern as the external organization is seemingly outside of the organization firewall.

Interfaces with an external organization almost always involve a well-defined API or industry messaging standard.

Interactions with external organizations are usually in one direction or of a higher latency than interfaces internal to an organization. One-directional interfaces would involve sending or receiving information without immediate responses required other than an acknowledgment. Most interactions with external organizations do not require sub-second response times. For those interactions with external organizations that do require very fast response times, such as the interactions with trading systems or exchanges, the message interaction model is well defined and the latency is well tuned between the organizations to ensure the fastest possible communications.

A SIDEBAR FROM THE AUTHOR—ON REAL-TIME DATA INTEGRATION ARCHITECTURE

Many organizations require real-time data integration capability, and every organization struggles with managing their interfaces and the overwhelming complexity inherent in doing so. It is easily demonstrated, as shown in the section on hub and spoke architecture, that without an enterprise data integration strategy the sheer number of interfaces quickly becomes unmanageable. The creation of business data hubs, such as data warehouses and master data hubs, helps to alleviate the potentially overwhelming complexity of managing data across an enterprise.

Every organization of even middle size should have an enterprise service bus to support, at least, real-time updates for the master data and for the data warehouse operational data stores, but also for the real-time movement of transactional data through the organization.

While working for an organization as the enterprise data architect, I proposed investment in an enterprise service bus architecture. My boss, who was the lead architect for the organization, counseled me not to be too disappointed if the technology strategy committee were not very enthusiastic about the idea, as they were not in general interested in future investment. At the presentation to the technology strategy committee, everyone on the committee ended up talking about how an integration strategy was crucial and about the vast number of issues and headaches they each routinely had to deal with associated with data integration problems. I ended up speaking very little as the members of the committee detailed all the justification the investment needed multifold.

Issues of moving and integrating data are, in fact, probably of high priority to most managers in both IT and business functions of every organization. These are tactical problems for which they will welcome a strategic solution. Attempting to solve the integration needs individually for each application in the organization is an overwhelming problem. It will cost the organization many times the cost of a strategic approach and an investment in an enterprise service bus and a canonical data model and even an enterprise metadata repository.

Big, Cloud,
Virtual Data

Introduction to Big Data Integration

18

INFORMATION IN THIS CHAPTER

Data integration and unstructured data

The discussion in the previous sections on batch data integration and real-time data integration addressed moving and integrating data stored in structured data structures, such as relational databases. However, databases only contain a small percentage of the data in an organization. The vast majority of organizational data is unstructured. It is important to be able to analyze unstructured data as well as integrate unstructured data with structured data.

A combination of recent breakthroughs in data integration technology and the knowledge developed in various data management disciplines such as business intelligence, data warehousing, and enterprise content management over the last two decades has culminated in many new and emerging data integration solutions. These new solutions do not replace the data integration techniques and solutions in current use but extend and refine what is already available.

Big data, cloud data, and data virtualization

Cloud architecture not only extends outside of the enterprise the data that needs to be integrated with internal data, but also introduces techniques and technologies around data and process replication. Big data technologies bring the benefits of distributed processing, with accompanying data integration challenges.

Data virtualization is the culmination of two decades of development and refinement in data management, incorporating solutions from batch data integration (ETL) and real-time data integration (ESB and hub and spoke), along with techniques from other data management disciplines and new technologies around unstructured data. Data virtualization servers don't replace the business intelligence tools, data warehouses, enterprise service buses, web services, or enterprise content management solutions, but build on them.

The technologies developed around cloud computing and big data recognize the shift of interest from the relatively small portion of data located in relational databases to leveraging the massive and varied available data located in both structured and unstructured form, in and out of the confines of the organization's data centers.

Cloud Architecture and Data Integration

19

INFORMATION IN THIS CHAPTER

Why is data integration important in the cloud?

Cloud solutions sound exceedingly attractive to management: It becomes unnecessary to manage all that infrastructure anymore, and management can quickly scale up (and down) volumes if needed.

Yet, in using cloud architecture, an organization should have concerns about latency caused by the physical distribution of the data and, even more importantly, the security of the data being stored in the cloud. Cloud solutions may be slower than local solutions because of potential delay caused by the speed of data traveling to and from the physical location of the cloud service provider, and the extra time needed to traverse additional security requirements for the data located in the cloud. How secure is data located in public cloud solutions? What are the legal ramifications of storing data in the geopolitical domains of the cloud vendors regarding privacy?

In general, the solutions for data integration regarding data in a public or private cloud are the same as for local data, since access to data is usually through virtual addressing. As long as the data consumer has sufficient access to the data located on the cloud, the data integration solutions are the same as for local data, with some additional concerns about latency and security.

Public cloud

With cloud solutions, organizations can rent computing power and software rather than buy it. This allows an organization to have additional servers, environments, and even applications with standard configurations available in minutes from a service provider operating out of a remote data center. Access to the rented computing environment is usually through an Internet protocol. There are many potential benefits possible for an organization using this kind of model; primary advantages are the agility it affords the organization to move very quickly and the cost savings of not having to buy and manage resources needed for infrequent peak demand. In Figure 19.1, the applications located within the organization data center passes data to and from an application located in a public cloud location.

Cloud security

Primary concerns around cloud solutions have to do with security. In the most basic situation, the cloud provider is serving many organizations within the same network environment. An organization could be concerned that their data might be hacked (accessed without permission) by another organization operating in the same area of the cloud data center. Even in cases where the cloud service provider has created a separate private cloud environment for an organization,

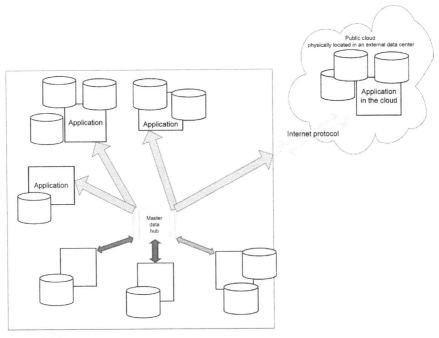

FIGURE 19.1

Integration with Cloud Applications.

operating on a separate network, behind a separate firewall, there must be concern for whether the service provider is providing adequate security from intruders.

The physical security provisions of the cloud service provider may be a concern, although since the provider is supporting security for all their customers and security is a differentiator, they are probably providing physical security which exceeds the internal capabilities of most individual organizations.

Additionally, the data security laws of the country where the cloud provider is operating its physical data center will be of concern to some organizations. For example, a Canadian company may not want to use a cloud service provider operating in the United States because its data could be subpoenaed by an American court.

Certain types of organizations will not be able to utilize public cloud solutions for their most private and sensitive information, such as the customer data from financial institutions or classified data from government organizations, but most organizations may find that the capabilities offered by cloud service providers are both less expensive and more secure than those they could support internally and would have many uses. Even the most security-conscious organization may find it useful to be able to create development environments in the cloud quickly, thus speeding up development of custom applications and familiarity with new vendor packages, while their internal organizations are provisioning environments within their own firewalls and data centers.

What many chief security officers are discovering, to their horror, is that cloud services are so easy and inexpensive to acquire that parts of their organizations may already have data out in public cloud environments without having been concerned with the issues of adequate security. Cloud services are so easy to obtain that the inventory of organizational data assets may suddenly be uncertain. Like data on laptops and mobile devices, data in the cloud is outside the organization's physical control and adds greater complexity to the problems of managing data security.

Cloud latency

There are three basic reasons that the speed of data integration with data housed in a cloud environment might be slower than data located in a local data center: the speed of the network infrastructure might be slower, extra time is needed to pass through the cloud security, and extra time is needed for the data to traverse to the physical location of the cloud data center.

The network infrastructure of an internal data center might or might not be constructed with faster connections than a cloud data center. Although an internal data center would probably be using expensive and fast components for their network, especially for production systems (i.e., fiber-optic network), it is likely that a cloud data center would also be investing in fast network infrastructure even though they would be using commodity (cheap) hardware. Delays may not be within the cloud data center but rather within the path data must take to get to and from the cloud data center.

Moving data to or from a cloud data center, or accessing data in a cloud data center, will involve passing through the extra security layers (firewall) around of the cloud data center, with the extra time that would be involved, even though that may be minimal.

What cloud service purveyors minimize in their advertising is that cloud data centers actually do exist in the real world in an actual physical location. Data passing to and from these physical data centers are limited by real-world constraints such as the speed constraints of how long it takes for digital information to pass to and from the physical site of the cloud data center. The physical distance of a cloud data center may have latency just as interaction between sites in different regions of the world will have latency. The physical distance from the cloud data center combined with the network infrastructure to and from the cloud data center may exacerbate any delay.

Although data integration solutions don't necessarily need to be different in including data from a public cloud as they would for local data integration, if very low latency is a requirement, it may be necessary to architect a data integration solution similar to the integration of geographically separated hubs of data located on different continents. Solutions such as database replication can be used to make up for latency of geographically distributed data, but the extra disk required may negate much of the savings benefits of the cloud solution.

Cloud redundancy

The servers and disk being used in most cloud configurations are commodity devices: inexpensive, easy to acquire, install, and configure. Therefore, the management of these commodity servers includes an assumption that there will be more frequent errors than in traditional in-house server configurations. That is, the mean time to failure is higher on commodity hardware. In order to create a fault-tolerant environment using commodity hardware, most cloud-oriented architectures use some form of data redundancy to enable smooth continuity of processing.

Cloud operating systems and data management systems, such as Hadoop, keep an odd number (as in not even) of copies of data. Additionally, data is usually distributed across multiple servers or nodes. When a server fails, processing falls back to one of the data copies. Having an odd number of copies allows for the nodes to compare versions of the data to verify that none of the copies have been corrupted or lost. The more critical the data, the greater the number of copies that are specified in the configuration, and, of course, the greater the rental cost.

The disk usually used in internal production environments is a "smart" disk with redundancy and fault tolerance built in, costing as much as 10 times that of commodity disk. Having three or five copies of data on commodity disk in a cloud environment should still be less expensive than internal disk, especially when including support costs.

More than with data kept internally, data kept in the cloud should include an inventory and auditing that no data has been lost or misplaced. With thousands and millions of commodity servers being constantly provisioned and deactivated, cloud services users should ensure that they have access to and are processing all the data they think they are. Also, when deactivating servers in the cloud, some concern should be taken to ensure that all data is entirely deleted prior to surrendering the servers.

Data Virtualization

A technology whose time has come

Data virtualization solutions allow an organization to present to their data consumers (people and systems) a real-time integrated view of data brought together from various locations and technologies and transformed into the format required. This is not a new business desire; rather, it's just that previous technical solutions tended to be too slow to make the real-time transformation and consolidation usable. Data warehouses were created primarily to be an instantiation of an integrated view of data because it wasn't feasible to do so in real time with a response time useful for business analysts. The most exciting aspect is that the information integrated and transformed by data virtualization includes unstructured sources as well as traditional structured sources of business intelligence.

Data virtualization is the culmination of all the techniques and technologies perfected in data integration and business intelligence over the last two decades. Data virtualization solutions are not meant to replace data warehouses but to build on top of them to integrate historical data in the data warehouse in real time with current data from various types of data structures that are local, remote,

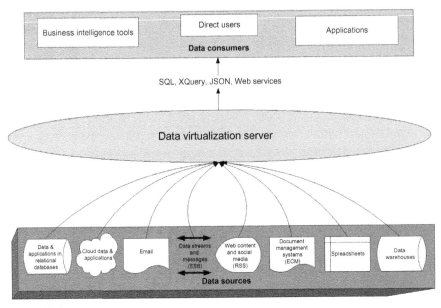

FIGURE 20.1

Data Virtualization Inputs and Outputs.

structured, unstructured, and transient and then to present them for instant use to the applications or users who need them in the format required.

The data integration server as depicted in Figure 20.1 provides a connection to various source data stores and technologies, transforming and integrating the data into a common view, and then providing the data in an appropriate format to an application, tool, or person in an expected form. This depiction is based on a presentation by Mike Ferguson at Enterprise Data World (Ferguson, 2012).

The data virtualization server can access data stores from the remote data of public cloud to the very local individual files, and differing technologies from mainframe indexed files, to documents, web content, and spreadsheets. The data virtualization server leverages all the lessons of data integration to most effectively access and transform the various data into a common view or views and builds on that with enterprise content management and metadata management to integrate structured and unstructured data. The organization's various data warehouses, document management systems, and Hadoop file stores are definitely among the sources to the data integration server.

The data consumers who use the integrated views from the data integration server are not just individuals, but more likely applications that leverage the integrated data for real-time decision making, or business intelligence tools to present the integrated data on screens and reports. The format of the data coming from the data integration server can be one that is most appropriate for the user, application, or tool: a web service, a relational database view, an XML file, a spreadsheet, etc.

Business uses of data virtualization
Business intelligence solutions

The results from data virtualization solutions will not return data faster than a data warehouse query. The reason is that a data warehouse is specially designed to return data quickly and a data virtualization solution needs to go through extra steps to transform and integrate the data. However, additional new types of data can be integrated more quickly with a data virtualization solution, and current data can be included and integrated real time.

Integrating different types of data

Data virtualization solutions are focused not just on the real-time aspect of data integration, which is an important goal in itself, but on the inclusion of a much broader set of data types than was previously included in business intelligence solutions.

Data virtualization solutions include the integration of data from unstructured data sources such as documents, e-mail, websites, social media posts, and data feeds, as well as the more traditional data from relational and other types of data-bases. In addition, data can be integrated from personal spreadsheets (where so much of an organization's data seems to live), files and databases on central servers, and data from the cloud and external sites. Data virtualization solutions can include data from real-time message solutions and data streams.

Quickly add or prototype adding data to a data warehouse

Data warehouses are not replaced by data virtualization solutions for two reasons: Data warehouses provide historical data, and data warehouses are faster. Data warehouses are a source for a data virtualization solution which makes both the data virtualization server and the data warehouse more powerful. A data warehouse may be a target from a data virtualization server, too, of data transformed from another source, including possibly unstructured sources into a structured format the data warehouse can use.

Data warehouses can be very powerful and useful solutions for an organization to use in data consolidation and reporting. However, it tends to take a very long time to add a new data source to a data warehouse, from concept to implementation. Data virtualization solutions can be used to quickly integrate additional data sources with data warehouse data to determine if the result is useful and to provide a temporary solution until the data source can be added to the data warehouse.

Data warehouses are designed for large amounts of data to be accessed and analyzed quickly. Data virtualization solutions must perform additional steps of collecting, transforming, and consolidating data from various data structures. Therefore, it is reasonable that data warehouse data retrieval will be faster than data virtualization retrieval.

Most data warehouses contain periodic snapshots of the state of data at certain points in time—historical data. These snapshots can be compared to one another to show historical changes or trends. This historical data is almost certainly not available in the operational systems and is difficult to show through a business intelligence or data virtualization solution without the data warehouse providing persistence or long-term storage of the historical data snapshots.

Present physically disparate data together

Besides the capability of transforming data in various formats into a consistent view, data virtualization solutions allow data from separate locations to be logically presented together (integrated). This is very useful when operational systems as well as reporting solutions have multiple instantiations in various locations, such as regional or business-line ERPs and data warehouses.

Leverage various data and models triggering transactions

The ultimate power of big data integration and management is in the ability to utilize not only various data types in analysis, but also results and process models that come out of that analysis to trigger real-time response to events. Data virtualization allows the integration of large amounts of data to be pumped through analytical and risk models to trigger both notification of organization decision makers and even the execution of transactions.

Data virtualization architecture
Sources and adapters

The data virtualization server architecture of course needs to include connections to the various data sources to be accessed. Data virtualization server products will provide adapters for the various types of sources: relational databases, files, documents, web content, and the like. Each particular data source to be accessed needs to be made known to the data virtualization server and the metadata imported and integrated.

Mappings and models and views

It is necessary to define the mappings from each data source to the common integrated data model or virtual view of the data defined in the data integration

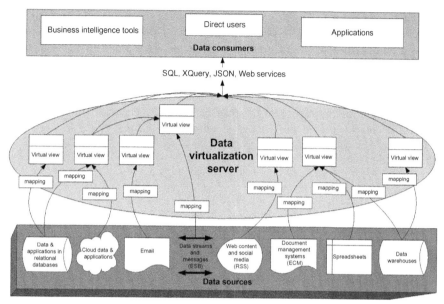

FIGURE 20.2

Data Virtualization Server Components.

server, the canonical model. This defines how the data from each source system needs to be transformed and reformatted in order to integrate the data.

It is an important but difficult task to define the common integrated data model (Ferguson, 2012) or the canonical data model for the organization. It is the agreed common virtual view of the integrated data of the organization. Both defining the canonical data model for the organization and mapping the data from the sources to the canonical model require both a business and technical understanding of the data.

It is very powerful to have one common virtual view in the data virtualization server that supports the needs of the entire organization, but it is also possible to have multiple various virtual views (van der Lans, 2012) of the data represented in the data virtualization server, as shown in Figure 20.2.

Integrating data from different technologies into a single view involves mapping the metadata attributes (or tags) from unstructured data and the key or index attributes from structured data to common attributes in the virtual views in the data virtualization server.

Transformation and presentation

From the virtual views or virtual tables (van der Lans, 2012) in the data virtualization server, the integrated data can be presented to the data consumer in the appropriate format. If the data consumer is an application, the data can be presented in the application programming interface (API) or web service (service oriented architecture service) format specific to the application. If the data consumer is a business intelligence tool or an application making a database call, the data can be presented in structured query language (SQL) or multidimensional expressions (MDX) format. Similarly, the data may be presented in XML or JSON if that is the preference of the data consumers. The transformation necessary to the data for presentation is just a technology reformat and is less difficult to automate than transforming data to the common canonical data model.

Big Data Integration

INFORMATION IN THIS CHAPTER

What is big data?

The definition of big data on Wikipedia is given as "data sets so large and complex that they become awkward to work with using on-hand database management tools." The term *big*, as well as this initial definition, imply that we are simply talking about the amount of data. However, big data also includes data of various types found outside of relational databases, such as documents, audio, video, and e-mail, as well as the increased speed and availability of data. Therefore, big data can be said to have dimensions of volume, variety, and velocity.

Big data dimension—volume

The volume of data that every organization needs to manage is now growing at a nonlinear pace. How much data "on-hand" database management tools can handle is a constantly expanding amount. "Traditional" relational database management systems can handle the volumes of structured, or relational, data of practically any organization.

Although existing relational database management tools can handle the onslaught of the additional data required, they may no longer be optimal for managing huge volumes nor may they be optimized for the various new use cases around big data. The traditional relational database management systems implement distributed storage solutions called grid or cluster storage where the data may be distributed across multiple storage structures randomly, based on the time received and stored, or based on other key pieces of information, such as the client or product. However, the cost of high-volume solutions in traditional database management systems does not scale linearly, and the volumes these solutions will support will ultimately hit an upper limit. "Big data" storage solutions such as those described in Chapter 19 on cloud architecture usually cost scale linearly and promise no ultimate upper limit to the volumes supported.

Massive parallel processing—moving process to data

When the volumes of data become extremely large, the normal paradigm of consolidating data prior to performing operations on the consolidated set of data becomes less attractive because of the time and extra disk needed to move and consolidate the data, plus the time it takes to parse linearly through a single, consolidated data set. A shift in paradigm for handling these massive volumes of data includes using parallel processing to simultaneously process against multiple chunks of data rather than attempting to process against a consolidated set. This includes leaving the data on the various distributed servers where it is already stored and distributing the query and update requests across the data sets, so-called "moving the process to the data" because we simultaneously perform the process on all the distributed data servers. Ultimately, the responses, results, and acknowledgments from the distributed servers have to be consolidated at the process distribution point, so there are important data integration steps, but the volume of the results to be integrated is much smaller than the original full set of data.

Hadoop and MapReduce

Massive parallel processing is not a new idea but has been around since the advent of low-cost central processing units and personal computers. It was not used more widely previously because of design rather than technology limitations. It is difficult to create algorithms and solve problems in a distributed manner versus central processing. However, the problem of "search" lends itself to distributed processing. The volumes of Internet data faced by social media organizations such as Google, Facebook, and Yahoo led to the creation of new tools that could solve standard problems using massive parallel processing. Distributed storage requires the use of distributed file systems (such as Hadoop) that recognize the data across the physical devices as being part of one data set, but still know where they are located in order to distribute processing.

Data for these social media sites is usually stored in a data set that is divided into a large number of physical devices using the Hadoop Distributed File system, which is not a relational database solution. Requests against the data are performed by dividing up the request into multiple queries that are sent out to act against the distributed data simultaneously, after which the results are consolidated. The primary software solution for this problem, called MapReduce, was originally developed by Google for its web search engine. The standard now used is an open-source solution called Hadoop MapReduce, developed in 2006 with funding by Yahoo. It became "production strength" (or "web scale") in 2008 and is currently hosted by Apache as part of the Hadoop Framework.

Hadoop and MapReduce solutions still need to distribute the processing requests and then re-integrate the various results. These distribution and consolidation steps are performed by MapReduce, which can also be categorized as an orchestration or even a data integration tool. The individual programmer defines what function needs to be performed against all the distributed data servers, and the underlying capabilities of MapReduce perform the distribution of the function and the consolidation of the results. Hadoop and MapReduce are usually implemented to perform in a batch mode. Real-time search and analysis is performed against the precalculated results sets, not the vast distribution of raw data. The data most frequently stored in Hadoop file structures are web logs and web data, which are usually considered to be unstructured.

Integrating with external data

There are vast amounts of data from outside an organization available to be integrated with an organization's internal data. Although many of these sources may have previously been available, at least in print form, the fact that it is now extremely simple, and in many cases free, to access petabytes of relevant information from external sources makes the leverage of this information necessary for every organization. There are huge data sets available from federal governments, such as data.gov from the United States federal government, from social media, and from information companies such as Google. The massive amounts of data that has been traditionally purchased from companies such as LexisNexis and Dun & Bradstreet are still available, adding more and more value to the purchased data to compete with what is available for free.

The integration issues on these vast amounts of available external data become exacerbated: Copying the external data internally is a challenge because of the amount of time, network bandwidth, and disk space this would require. The processes can't be distributed to the external servers because these are owned by another organizational entity. Therefore, it is necessary, in general, to read and process the external data and transform the data to the format for use by the organization, only keeping the data needed for integration with internal data. Decisions about the data life cycle are particularly critical for data from external sources: How much of it is needed? Does it need to be persisted (stored locally)? How long does it need to be retained? Of course, these questions need to be answered for an organization's internal data as well, though frequently the default answer has been to keep all the internal data, which is not usually an option with external data.

Visualization

The presentation of big data is a challenge because with the large volume, variety, and velocity of the information, presenting detailed information becomes difficult or inappropriate for human consumption. Presentation in visual form frequently provides the capability to summarize vast amounts of information into a format that is conducive to human consumption and that may provide the ability to drill down to a further level of detail, if requested.

Big data dimension—variety
Types of data

The amount or volume of data is not the only aspect that makes data "big." Frequently, when considering what data is available for analysis, organizations have solely looked at data stored in relational databases. Now, organizations have the ability to analyze data stored in files, documents, e-mail, audio and video files, and a vast array of database types in addition to relational databases. In addition, huge amounts of external data are available that are not entirely "structured" such as social media data from Twitter, Facebook, YouTube, and blogs.

Integrating different types of data

The key to integrating the different types of data is to use metadata that "tags" unstructured data with attributes that can be linked. Thus, more "unstructured data", like images, are "tagged" with metadata that identifies, for example, what an image is or who a person is in an image or audio file, as well as when and where the data was created, updated, and accessed. Documents and e-mail can be indexed by words, phrases, and names found in the text or associated with the data. Logical organization of the information is made through taxonomies (hierarchies) and ontologies (groupings). These "tags" on unstructured data can be linked to keys and indexes in databases, thus bringing the unstructured and structured data together.

An example of integrating data of various types may be that, for a customer, an organization has document images of contracts with that customer; contact information and transaction data in databases; e-mail with and about that customer; audio files with the customer's instructions and service calls; and video of the customer visiting the organization's office. All this information on the customer may be integrated and available to the customer service representative when a customer calls the organization.

INTERVIEW WITH AN EXPERT: WILLIAM MCKNIGHT ON HADOOP AND DATA INTEGRATION

Following is an interview with William McKnight on the importance and use of Hadoop in data integration.

William McKnight is an expert on data management and has been working with data integration for many years, populating data warehouses, data warehouse appliances, and master data management hubs. Recently, he has been working with data integration solutions to populate Hadoop.

What is Hadoop?

Hadoop makes "source data-database-data access" economical for the management of large-scale Web logs and other forms of big data. Hadoop, an important part of the NoSQL (Not Only SQL) movement, usually refers to a family of open-source products, including the Hadoop Distributed File System (HDFS) and MapReduce. The Hadoop family of products extends into a rapidly growing set of tools and utilities. Although open source, many vendors have created some closed-source additional capabilities and/or added Hadoop support in their product set. Other open-source Hadoop family products include Avro, Pig, Hive, HBase, Zookeeper, and Sqoop. The Hadoop File System (HDFS) part of the Hadoop project is like a "big data" extract and load (EL) tool with good data-screening ability. HDFS runs on a large cluster of commodity nodes.

How is Data Integration (i.e., moving and transforming data) Related to Hadoop?

As a nonoperational platform or file system, Hadoop must receive its data from another source. Given the enormous volume of the data—and the trade-off that not falling behind takes the place of delays to clean the data—little is done to transform the data being loaded into HDFS, but the data is largely just loaded into the Hadoop environment in its raw form.

Have you Seen any Projects Using Hadoop Where Data Integration Issues Led to Significant Problems? Or Where Insufficient Focus Was Put on Data Integration Issues?

Analyzing Hadoop data without the perspective of other corporate data, currently maintained mostly in relational systems, is very limiting. Master data management can take the value of this data in Hadoop up exponentially, but tools like data virtualization must be available to integrate data between Hadoop and relational database management systems.

What Kinds of Tools or Technologies are Used to Support Data Integration with Hadoop?

- Traditional ETL Vendors
- Data Virtualization
- Data Integration for the Masses
- Federated Big Data Analysis

How do you Think the Area of Hadoop and Data Integration is Changing? Are the Tools Supporting it Changing? Where do you Think this Area is Going to?

Hadoop is emerging as data integration is changing, and indeed Hadoop is influencing that direction. Data integration is becoming more personal and accessible. Companies are also looking at balancing physical movement with the implementation of virtualization across heterogeneous data stores. However, with the vast increase in data store types that add value, data is increasingly becoming decentralized, continues to be replicated, is doubling every 18 months, and is increasingly seen as a competitive differentiator. As such, its movement will continue to be important. Each shop will have its numerous specific points of data integration. Every organization will approach its information architecture uniquely. There is a need in every organization for a robust, enterprise-ready, fully deployable, low-cost integration tool. Standardizing a single data integration tool or suite across the organization will be best so that harmony of skills, practices, and experiences can be maintained across the enterprise.

Big data dimension—velocity

Because many devices such as sensors, mobile phones, and geospatial tracking (GPS), are getting cheaper and ubiquitous, there is now an expectation that this information will be stored and made available. Tagging inventory and assets with radio transponders allows a constant trail of location information on manufactured goods. People voluntarily tag themselves with mobile phone location information and their cars with GPS devices and toll sensors. In short, a huge raft of additional sensor data is now expected to be available for analysis.

Not only is data coming at us faster, but the expectation is that the organization will be able to use the data immediately to make decisions. The velocity aspect of big data lies not only in the speed of incoming data but also in the speed of expected use.

Streaming data

Streams of data are now available from various sources internal and external to every organization, both free and at a cost. Even though the cost of disk space is very low compared to what was in the past, the cost of storing this vast amount of data may still quickly become unwarranted. Every organization needs to make decisions about the retention period for the various available data streams. For data that does not contain confidential or private information, cloud storage solutions may provide support for temporary, inexpensive persistence of the data streams with defined redundancy and retention schedules.

Sensor and GPS data

Internal data may be available from sensors on people and physical assets, such as inventory and trucks. Real-time sensor data can be used for real-time decision making, such as fast inventory and detouring product delivery in support of higher business priorities or issues. Historical sensor data can be used to improve processes such as standard delivery routes, gasoline consumption, and productivity. This type of internal sensor data is available to most organizations. The availability of general sensor data and sensor data specific to individual industries and businesses has made possible a potential golden age of analytics.

Social media data

Also available to organizations is the consumer data available on social media sites. Most organizations monitor data referencing themselves as well as their competitors on Facebook, Twitter, LinkedIn, and major blog sites in support of customer service and their organizational reputation.

Traditional big data use cases

Certain big data problems and use cases are common to every organization, such as e-mail, contracts and documents, web data, and social media data. In addition, almost every industry has specific cases where they have big data management problems to solve. Many industries have always had to deal with huge volumes and varied types of data. Organizations in the telecommunications industry must keep track of the huge network of nodes through which communications can pass and the actual activity and history of connections. Finance has to process both the history of prices of financial products and the detailed history of financial transactions. Organizations in airplane manufacturing and operation must track the history of every part and screw of every airplane and vehicle planned and operated. Publishing organizations must track all the components of documents through the development versions and production process. Interestingly, pharmaceutical firms have similar strict document management requirements for their drug submissions to the FDA in the United States, and comparable requirements in other countries; thus, for pharmaceutical firms advanced document management capabilities are a core competency and a traditional "big data" problem.

More big data use cases

Big data use cases are emerging in every industry and organization where technology solutions can now perform functions with vast amounts of information and in real-time situations that were not previously available.

Health care

The ability to analyze vast amounts of information allows breakthrough analytical capabilities in health care at the individual and macro levels. It is now possible to analyze an entire individual human DNA sequence and compare it against those of other individuals and groups. The current relatively low cost to perform individual DNA analysis (thousands of dollars) has made this tool accessible to a substantial number of people compared to the initial cost of millions of dollars a few years ago after the first full human genome was analyzed.

Analysis of the health care data of millions of individuals and groups is now a routine capability that may lead to making great strides in public health administration as well as individual health care. The New York Times carried an article recently ("Mining Electronic Records for Revealing Health Data" by Peter Jaret, January 15, 2013) positing that analysis of electronic health records may be able to provide data to support costly clinical trial data collection, providing vastly more data for data analysis of theories in health care as well as much less costly data.

Logistics

Big data use cases in manufacturing include those in the product development process itself as well as in inventory and distribution. The low cost of sensors makes constant monitoring of product manufacturing regarding quality and productivity a best practice. Identification tags broadcasting unique product identifiers are now of relatively low cost. They enable a constant monitoring of inventory and the ability to make real-time distribution adjustments.

National security

Some really fascinating big data use cases are emerging within the area of public security. Telecommunications information analysis has been a traditional function of law enforcement in monitoring communications to or from specific individuals. Now, the actual contents of vast numbers of audio conversations can be monitored for the use of specific words or phrases such as "bomb." Networks of associates of known and potential individuals who pose a security threat can be developed from the telephone history of billions of phone calls. That information now includes the location of where calls were made and received as well as where the mobile phone is currently located.

Leveraging the power of big data—real-time decision support
Triggering action

Important big data use cases are moving from analysis of vast amounts of historical data to analysis of vast amounts of current data that can be used to make real-time decisions.

Changes in available data in the area of utilities and traffic control are making historical data analysis fascinating and real-time data analysis amazing. Practically every vehicle on the road is now equipped with a GPS or other tracking device, making it possible to perform traffic analysis at the individual vehicle behavior level and macro analysis of the combined behavior of all the vehicles. This information is being used real time to manage traffic lights and long term to affect infrastructure investment.

The reduced cost of sensors has made it cost effective for utilities to have vast numbers of sensors in place providing environmental and use data that can be analyzed and acted upon in real time plus stored and analyzed for process improvement. Models that have been created from big data of utility grid behavior just prior to an emergency can be used in the future in real time to automatically trigger utilities to cut off, bypass, or obtain additional resources.

Risk management calculations in financial services, using a vast amount of historical information on holdings and prices and price changes, can provide worst case scenarios and probabilities concerning financial portfolios. The models created from these calculations are then used in real-time decision support, triggering warnings and automatic trading based on streaming pricing data.

Financial institutions model every individual's buying and use behavior. Then when the individual's activity falls outside of the regular pattern, warnings are automatically distributed to the individual and client support specialists to verify that the activity is not fraudulent.

In a less frightening direction, big data analysis of customer behavior for buying and renting movies, books, and clothes can now yield recommendations to individual customers. The following phrase is now common: "other customers like you also purchased . . .". Even analysis of social media contents of individuals and the networks can be used to recommend movies, music, and other entertainment.

Speed of data retrieval from memory versus disk

Faced with the increased velocity of big data decision-making requirements, small real-time delays in incoming data processing, data access, and response can be significant. Once again, the lower costs of fast disk and memory can be utilized to take advantage of big data velocity.

A simplistic way of thinking about the relative time to retrieve data is that if it takes a certain amount of time in nanoseconds to retrieve something in memory, then it will be approximately 1000 times that to retrieve data from disk (milliseconds). Depending on the infrastructure configuration, retrieving data over a local area network (LAN) or from the Internet may be ten to 1000 times slower than that. If we load our most heavily used data into memory in advance, or something that behaves like memory, then processing of that data should be speeded up by multiple orders of magnitude. Using solid-state disk for heavily used data can achieve access and update response times similar to having data in memory. Computer memory, as well as solid-state drives, though not as inexpensive as traditional disk, are certainly substantially less expensive than they used to be and are getting cheaper all the time.

Why is this concept relevant to data integration? These differences in processing time are changing the way many applications are designed and the way analysis and analytics are performed. Traditional data analysis would pull together data (data integration) into a report that an analyst would view and derive insight from. In many situations, a model would be created to attempt to predict future behavior or manage risk. The model would have to be loaded with large amounts of historical data.

The models generated through traditional analysis or through big data analysis are now being used against the large volume and velocity of data available in real time, in addition to historical data, and actions are being triggered immediately based on the results. Risk calculations are used to immediately trigger actions based on price fluctuations. Customer sentiment calculations immediately trigger response. Current sales information can immediately trigger inventory redistribution. Traffic volume can immediately trigger additional support.

From data analytics to models, from streaming data to decisions

The ultimate goal of big data then is to tap into the vast amount of information available to make better real-time decisions.

Large volumes of data of various types and sources are analyzed for patterns that identify potential risks and opportunities for an organization. This analysis is probably performed by highly skilled data analysis specialists such as data scientists in a flexible analytical environment called an analytics sandbox. The analysts create process and event models that identify opportunities to be leveraged or risks to be avoided.

The models are then integrated with real-time streaming data that, when certain patterns or situations occur, trigger warnings and transactions to respond immediately to the highlighted situation.

These opportunities and risks are currently available in every industry and organization. All consumer organizations, for example, monitor social media sources for feedback that triggers action. Organizations that don't immediately respond to negative information in social media could quickly find their reputation in crisis.

Big data architecture

Tools and technologies for big data include those for other enterprise information management activities: enterprise content management (or document management), data warehousing and business intelligence (including data visualization), data analytics, data integration, metadata management, and data virtualization. The need for tools in support of these capabilities becomes more important with big data because the volumes are usually beyond a human manageable scale and require some degree of automation.

Figure 21.1 depicts the logical pieces involved not only in big data integration but in big data solution architecture as well.

Operational systems and data sources

The sources of data in a big data architecture may include not only the traditional structured data from relational databases and application files, but unstructured data files that contain operations logs, audio, video, text and images, and e-mail, as well as local files such as spreadsheets, external data from social media, and real-time streaming data from sources internal and external to the organization.

Intermediate data hubs

The organization is probably using intermediate data hubs for structured data (data warehouses, marts, and operational data stores), various documents and files (email and enterprise content management servers), social media and web data (Hadoop), and master data, with various flavors, implementations, locations, and configurations of all of these.

Existing data warehouses, data marts, and analytic appliance implementations are an important part of the full big data architecture, although these data structures are probably only storing structured data. Integrating the data in these various warehouse stores with other types of data and current operational data is where the power of big data analysis can be achieved.

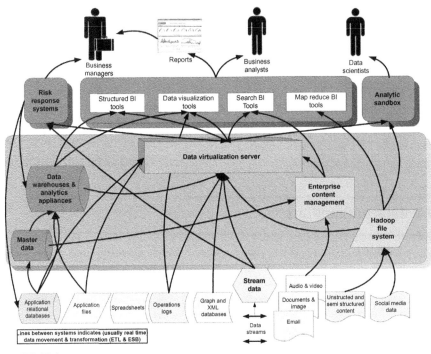

FIGURE 21.1

Big Data Architecture Components.

Various data streams will be coming in to the big data environment, and some of it will persist, for however long specified by data type and content, as appropriate to the organization. Cloud-based solutions and Hadoop may be appropriate for temporary persistence of this type of high-volume, low-value data.

Business intelligence tools

Structured business intelligence

Along with the data warehouse data stores are the traditional business intelligence tools that operate primarily on structured data in relational databases. The traditional business intelligence tools become more powerful than ever when fed data in an appropriate structured format from the unstructured data sources through the data virtualization server.

Search business intelligence

Critical to big data architecture is the inclusion of tools for managing documents and e-mail, including business intelligence tools focused on analyzing this data, which is commonly referred to as "search" type of analysis. The search analysis tools can access across data of many types and in many locations.

Hadoop and MapReduce business intelligence

In many cases, "big data" and Hadoop are used as synonyms. As part of the Hadoop solution set, MapReduce is generally used for orchestration and analysis of the data stored in the Hadoop File System.

Visualization

Data visualization tools for presenting massive amounts of information are used against data from most of the intermediate data hubs, including data warehouses, data streams, and Hadoop.

Data virtualization server

The data virtualization server will be a central and critical component in the big data architecture, as it facilitates integrating data from various technologies and sources and formatting for use by various data consumer tools and applications.

Batch and real-time data integration tools

Moving and presenting the data between data structures and tools in the big data architecture can utilize both batch (ETL) and real-time (ESB) data integration tools, as well as the capabilities of the various components, including the data virtualization server, MapReduce applications, and business intelligence tools.

Analytic sandbox

Big data architecture will usually include an area set aside for analysis of the available data sources by analytic process specialists. The analytic sandbox allows the review of large amounts of data from various sources and of various types by specialists using sophisticated tools to identify patterns in the data. The analysts produce reports of results and process models to be used for real-time decision making.

Risk response systems/recommendation engines

The ultimate goal of big data is to leverage the vast information for real-time decision making. The risk response systems use complex event processing (CEP) and the process models developed by the data analysts and data scientists to respond to real-time information and trigger warnings to business managers as well as to trigger transactions to respond to opportunities and risks highlighted during the big data analysis processes.

INTERVIEW WITH AN EXPERT: JOHN HADDAD ON BIG DATA AND DATA INTEGRATION

Following is an interview with John Haddad on Big Data and Data Integration.

John Haddad is Director of Product Marketing for Big Data at Informatica Corporation. He has over 25 years' experience developing and marketing enterprise applications. Prior to Informatica, John was Director of Product Management and Marketing at Right Hemisphere, held various positions in R&D and Business Development at Oracle Corporation, and began his career as a scientific programmer at Stanford University.

How do you Define "Big Data"?

Big data is the confluence of big transaction data (e.g., RDBMS), big interaction data (e.g., social data, web logs, sensor devices, e-mails), and big data processing (e.g., Hadoop) primarily resulting from the adoption of social, mobile, and cloud computing. Big data can drive rapid innovation by analyzing and extracting value from more data, more types of data, and at faster speeds.

How is Data Integration (i.e., moving and transforming data) Related to Big Data?

It turns out that 80% of the work in a big data project involves data integration. When I speak about data integration, I'm referring to the ability to access, parse, normalize, standardize, integrate, cleanse, extract, match, classify, mask, and deliver data. According to D. J. Patil in his book *Data Jujitsu*, "80% of the work in any data project is in cleaning the data." And in a recent study involving 35 data scientists from 25 companies one of the participants stated, "I spend more than half my time integrating, cleansing, and transforming data without doing any actual analysis. Most of the time I'm lucky if I get to do any 'analysis' at all." (Kandel et al. Enterprise Data Analysis and Visualization: An Interview Study. IEEE Visual Analytics Science and Technology (VAST), 2012). In other words, before you can do anything useful with big data, you need to integrate it. This is because big data is coming from so many different types of sources and in many different formats.

How and Why is Data Moved for Big Data?

Not only is there much more data, but there are many different types of data sources in various types of structures and formats. Data is being generated and consumed at a massive scale from both inside and outside the enterprise from customer and supplier transactions, the Internet, and social, cloud, and sensor devices to name but a few. To extract value from big data requires that data be moved from the point of origin and source systems to big data platforms that integrate, analyze, and deliver value from all this raw data.

Are There Other Aspects of Data Integration in Big Data Besides Moving and Transforming Data?

Yes, in some cases you may want to avoid moving data by using data virtualization. Data virtualization allows you to create a data abstraction layer that hides the underlying complexity of the data sources. From this data abstraction layer you can decide whether to federate across the data sources or move the combined data into a physical target.

Another key aspect of data integration is metadata management and data governance. Metadata management creates a semantic layer to better understand the data and support data governance initiatives.

Are There Different Data Integration Considerations for Structured Data Integration and Unstructured Data Integration?

There are; however, I find it more useful to delineate between traditional row-column formatted relational and flat file data versus multistructured (e.g., hierarchical, graph) and unstructured data (e.g., text). The former in many cases can only be processed at a scale using traditional data platforms (e.g., RDBMS), while the latter can be stored and processed more cost-effectively using emerging NoSQL technologies such as Hadoop. You can also draw a distinction between high-density, high-value data (e.g., typically stored in RDBMS) and low-density raw data (e.g., web logs, social media text) to help decide where to best store, integrate, and process data.

Have you Seen any Big Data Projects Where Data Integration Issues Led to Significant Problems?

Yes, when data integration is not done properly, it all too often results in project delays, failed projects, and low end-user adoption and can directly impact the business resulting in poor customer service, inferior products, inefficient operations, and bad decision making. Consider the implications of incomplete, inconsistent, inaccurate, and untimely data being delivered to the business. The impact can be inconsistent customer experience across order channels, declining loyalty due to delivery delays or billing errors, or lost revenue from lack of optimal cross-sell/up-sell.

Have you Had Experiences Where Particular Attention was Paid to Data Integration in Big Data?

The best practice process for data integration in big data projects is one that involves the ability to access and ingest, parse and prepare, discover and profile, transform and cleanse, and extract and deliver data. As I mentioned earlier, 80% of the work in a big data project is data integration. For example, large global banks use data integration for big data projects related to fraud detection, risk and portfolio analysis, investment recommendations, regulatory compliance, and proactive customer engagement. I like what Amazon CTO Werner Vogels said during his keynote, entitled "Data Without Limits" at the Cebit trade show earlier this year: "Big data is not only about analytics, it's about the whole pipeline. So when you think about big data solutions you have to think about all the different steps: collect, store, organize, analyze and share."

Have you Had Experiences Where Data Integration Was Neglected on a Big Data Project? Why do you Think Data Integration Was Neglected?

Yes, it is usually neglected because of a quick and dirty approach to integration that takes the path of least resistance. These projects don't fully consider the scope and necessary requirements to support and maintain big data projects in production as data volumes grow and new data types are added. Organizations need a data integration platform that can scale linearly, provides 24×7 reliability, supports an architecture flexible to change, and provides tools that enhance productivity and facilitate collaboration.

Are There Special Considerations Around the Movement of Metadata for Big Data?

I would say that there are special considerations related to metadata for big data in general. Bear in mind that not all data is modeled on ingestion with big data projects. Raw interaction data (e.g., social data, web logs, sensor devices, e-mails, etc.) tends to be processed as schema-on-read as opposed to schema-on-write. Therefore there is an inherent lack of metadata in big data projects. This is where the importance of data governance plays a critical role in big data projects. Metadata can be acquired through data discovery (e.g., domains, relationships) and curated (e.g., normalized, cleansed) through data stewardship. Some metadata can be accumulated automatically as data is accessed, integrated, analyzed, and used throughout the enterprise. For example, data lineage for compliance audits and usage patterns can be automatically acquired with some data integration tools. There are different types of metadata (technical, business, operational) that are very useful in managing big data projects so as to enhance search, simplify data audits, ensure trust, improve collaboration, reduce rework, and increase security.

What Kinds of Tools or Technologies are Used to Support Data Integration for Big Data?

Big data needs a data integration platform optimized to support a heterogeneous data environment, including productivity tools, one that scales for production use and multiple projects and makes it easier to support and maintain projects throughout the project life cycle. Big data projects require data integration tools that provide consistent and reliable connectivity for both transaction and interaction data, prebuilt ETL and data quality transformations, parsing libraries (parsers), a visual integrated development environment (IDE) to build data flows, and data profiling. Organizations need a data integration platform that supports all volumes and types of data and also supports real-time and batch processing through data replication, data streaming, and complex event processing (CEP). Data integration should be considered as part of a complete big data reference architecture that also includes MDM.

When Might you Use Batch Data Integration versus Real-time Data Integration in a Big Data Project? Do you Think it is Worthwhile to Have Both Batch and Real-time Data Integration Solutions Working with a Big Data Solution?

Batch integration is primarily used to preprocess large volumes of data for analytics, and identify patterns and trends that can be exploited by the business. Business value is derived from batch integration by processing more data faster and more types of data. Real-time data integration has a couple of uses: to smooth out the big data processing load by capturing and integrating only changed data to avoid unnecessarily staging data and lengthy batch windows and to proactively respond to events based on situational awareness. Both batch and real-time data integration can provide some very interesting big data solutions. For example, it is common in fraud detection to analyze a very large corpus of historical data in batch that identifies patterns of fraud and uses real-time data integration to establish situational context and determine in real time the likeliness that a fraud event is happening, which in turn generates an alert.

How do you Think the Area of Big Data is Changing? Where do you Think This Area is Heading?

The technology side of big data is changing rapidly. However, I'm afraid (as often is the case with new technologies and trends) that the people and process side of the equations is not adopting best practices fast enough to assimilate the advantages big data has to offer. Ultimately, success depends on the business and IT working much more efficiently and in collaboration with each other. The formation of data science teams devoted to managing data as an asset to create innovative data products and services requires a variety of skills, some of which need to be acquired from outside or through additional training. Big data projects deviate from traditional business intelligence in that organizations need a more aligned top-down business technology strategy that continuously explores ways to maximize the return on data, monetize data assets by introducing new products and services, and improve business operations. We can expect to see executive sponsorship of data science teams aligned with strategic business initiatives (e.g., increase customer acquisition and retention).

Do you Think the Technologies for Supporting Big Data, especially Around Data Integration, are Changing?

Big data technologies are changing and evolving rapidly. The open-source community and commercial vendors are working with their customers to mature newly emerging technologies and make sure these technologies work with existing data management infrastructure. We will see more purpose-built applications based on common design patterns (e.g., recommendation engines) and vertical specific big data use-cases (e.g., risk and portfolio analysis, predicting patient outcomes, vehicle telematics). A lot of new technologies require specialized skills that add to the complexity of big data projects. So we will see vendors begin to integrate these technologies and create abstraction layers that hide the underlying complexities of these technologies.

Conclusion to Managing Data in Motion

INFORMATION IN THIS CHAPTER

Data integration architecture
Why data integration architecture?

Every organization should have a data integration strategy as the volumes and complexity of the data they are required to manage escalates rapidly. Without a data integration strategy the natural complexity of interfaces between applications quickly becomes unmanageable. The data integration strategy may be part of the data management strategy or simply part of the technology strategy, but it should include batch, real-time, and big data integration management.

This chapter will review the components of a data integration strategy.

Data integration life cycle and expertise

The project life cycle of any data integration project is similar to the flow of a batch data integration project, as depicted in Figure 5.2. Additionally, as in Figure 22.1, a data discovery process or impact analysis may be needed early in the analysis to determine where and how much data will be impacted by the project. This depiction does not include the specification or acquisition of data integration tools or additional disk or servers. Data discovery is usually a necessity for most data integration projects, including master data management and data archiving. It is usually less of a need for data conversion and data warehousing projects, where the sources may be known. The need for a data discovery phase is becoming even more relevant with the advent of big data volumes and complexity.

Identifying the right resources to specify and code data integration solutions has presented a conundrum from the early days of batch ETL development. Designing overall solutions requires a combination of specific technical knowledge of data integration technology and tools, high-level business process flow, and detailed business data understanding. It is necessary to develop overall data integration design using a combination of people working together with either a technical or business resource leading the effort. Specifying detailed interfaces requires a combination of detailed tool knowledge, detailed technical data knowledge, and detailed business data knowledge. Once again, the effort may be led by either a business or technology person. Coding solutions requires expertise in the chosen data integration technology and tools, but with detailed specification approved by the business experts on the source and target data and the application developers supporting the source and target systems.

Best practice and consensus is that the creation of a Center of Excellence for data integration within an organization's data or information technology function is most productive for developing and managing data integration solutions, where the participants have expertise on the life cycle of data integration development projects as well as expertise in the data integration technologies. Requests for interfaces or data integration solutions can be made to the center of excellence, which can then involve the necessary business and technical expertise from the organization as well as ensure that solutions follow organization policies, standards, and best practices.

Security and privacy

As with all data and application implementation in organizations these days, data integration development must ensure that the overall data integration architecture, individual data integration solutions, and all data integration development

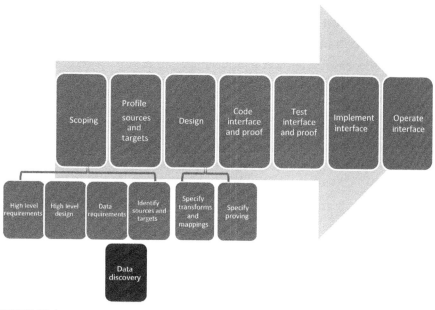

FIGURE 22.1

Data Integration Project Life Cycle.

processes support organizational policies, standards, and best practices in security and privacy.

This can be particularly challenging for data integration projects starting with the need to perform data discovery and profiling of real production data. It is usually necessary to negotiate with the information security organization and have data discovery and profiling performed by individuals with appropriate access authority, which may mean assigning more expensive individuals or even training individuals who have the appropriate authority to perform the profiling tasks.

Since one of the main functions of data integration is moving data, it is required that all data in motion (or between persistent data stores) be adequately secured and, if necessary, encrypted, to certify that it can't be accessed by unauthorized persons or systems.

For data that is presented through data integration solutions, either through copies or views, it is necessary to ensure that all individuals accessing the data have the authority to do so. Moreover, any systems or applications who are given copies or access to data should only allow access to individuals and systems that have the appropriate authority. Since any system that gives access to data has the responsibility to manage appropriate access authority, it is necessary to negotiate with source applications to get access; it is also necessary to ensure that target applications only allow appropriate access.

Data integration engines
Operational continuity

The processing engines for data integration are operational systems; hence they have to be up and running to operate and orchestrate the system interfaces. These systems have to have immediate system support available and be included in the disaster recovery tier of the most critical systems being integrated.

The data integration engines support, by design, across multiple technology environments, operating systems, database management systems, and vendor applications.

ETL engine

For batch data integration, which is used to support data warehousing, data archiving, and data conversions, among other things, the organization may be operating one or more ETL engines. There are possibly more than one because the organization may have multiple data warehouses that were developed separately using various ETL technology solutions or may even be using the same technology but multiple instances. Figure 22.2 depicts the basic batch data integration architecture supported by the ETL engine.

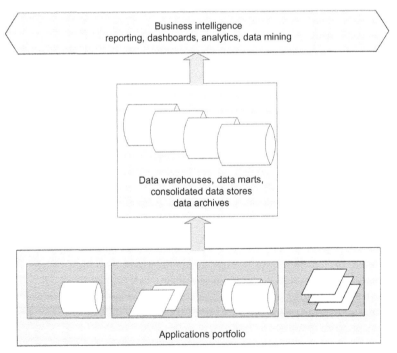

FIGURE 22.2

Batch Data Integration Architecture.

Batch ETL engines are most frequently used to load data into data warehouses and extract out for business intelligence, analytical, and reporting tools.

Enterprise service bus

Real-time interfaces are most frequently implemented using an enterprise service bus (ESB) to orchestrate the interactions between applications and systems.

Real-time interfaces are used to support master data management (moving data into and out of the master data hubs real time) as well as the movement of transactional data updates between applications. Figure 22.3 shows the real-time data integration architecture supported by an enterprise service bus.

The enterprise service bus implements the movement of data between applications and the transformation of data from the specific source application format to the common canonical model format and to the format of the target systems. The enterprise service bus supports the interaction patterns of "publish and subscribe" and "request and reply".

Supporting the enterprise service bus are local utilities to handle data movement, event monitoring, and transaction processing middleware.

Data virtualization server

The data virtualization server provides real-time integration of data from various technologies and types, both structured and unstructured. It pulls the data and reformats into an integrated view and then presents in appropriate formats for various consumers, including people and systems, without staging or instantiating the intermediate data. Figure 22.4 depicts the data flow of a data virtualization server.

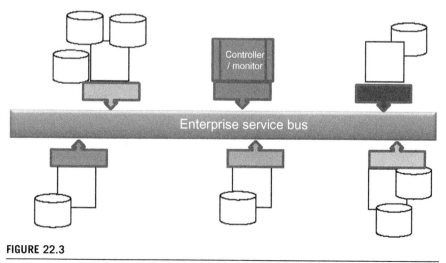

FIGURE 22.3

Real-Time Data Integration Architecture.

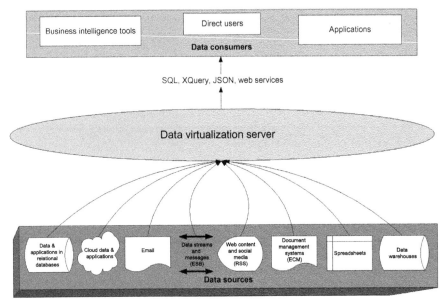

FIGURE 22.4

Data Virtualization Server.

A data virtualization server may utilize data from an ETL engine or an enterprise service bus as a source, as well as structured and unstructured data hubs and operational systems, and may provide data to a data warehouse or an operational data store as a target, as well as various operational applications and business intelligence tools.

Data movement

The data integration engines generally use the utility capabilities of the various environments where the data and applications are located to perform the actual movement of data, if necessary, including schedulers, database monitors and triggers, business process and transaction management middleware, and other process and data movement utilities.

Data integration hubs

Figure 22.5 depicts the components of a big data environment.

Managing data integration through hubs helps to simplify management of the organization's interfaces. Data Hubs can bring the number of interfaces from being

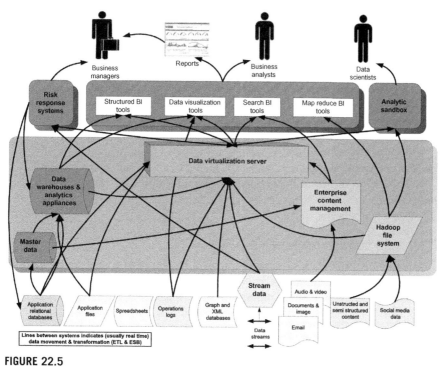

FIGURE 22.5

Big Data Architecture.

an exponential function of the number of applications to being a linear function of the number of applications. The business-oriented hubs of master data, data warehousing, and data archiving strongly support making enable management of the portfolio of application interfaces. The hubs depicted in Figure 22.5 are known by the business areas; this is in contrast to the hub-and-spoke approach to real-time data integration, which is a more technical approach to managing interfaces and may not be known outside of the information technology organization.

Master data

Master data is the critical key data in the organization such as customers, products, employees, vendors, financial accounts, and reference data. A master data hub provides a central location for managing and providing master data to the organization. A master data hub that is supported using batch data integration can provide support for business intelligence and reporting functions, but usually it is necessary to have real-time data integration to support managing master data and supplying updates to operational applications.

Data warehouse and operational data store

Data warehouses are an integrated hub of data that can be used to support business analysis and reporting. Many organizations actually implement multiple data warehouses to support different geographies or functions within the organization. Again, a data warehouse helps to make data integration in an organization manageable by providing a central hub of data to be used for reporting and analysis. All the consumers who want to access that data can get it from a single place rather than having to go to various operational applications directly.

Data warehouses are usually updated using batch data integration, and if real-time consolidated information is needed, then an operational data store would be created which would consolidate operational application data using real-time data integration.

Enterprise content management

Unstructured data objects such as documents, images, audio, and video may be managed through a central enterprise content management repository. This type of repository serves the same purpose as the structured data hubs, by enabling consolidated management of many types of unstructured data across the organization.

Data archive

When data is no longer needed for operational processing, it may be more cost effective to archive the data for some period of time to a less expensive data store until it is certain that the organization no longer needs it or while it is required to be maintained by regulations. Data archival may also be necessary when an application is retired or replaced.

Data backups are specific to a particular application, technology, and schema, and may not be easily recoverable if the data structures are modified or the application is no longer in operation. Additionally, providing a central capability that will manage archived data and make it accessible across all the applications in the organization and various data types is more cost effective and flexible.

Metadata management

Metadata management is becoming a critical capability within data integration and within most data management areas. Metadata allows the linking or integration of structured and unstructured data types together. Also, it is quickly becoming impossible to hand-craft metadata with the volumes and types of data being managed, and it is becoming a necessity to have tools that can automatically create much of the needed metadata, and not just capture the metadata created during the development and operation processes.

Data discovery

Data discovery is becoming a necessary capability as the volume of data in organizations is growing exponentially, making it almost impossible to know in advance the full impact of potential changes, development, or interest.

The most advanced data discovery products can identify where data is located using the names of fields and tags, as well as the actual content of the data structures.

Data profiling

Data profiling is a required function in advance of every data-related development project.

Once the general location of the data of interest has been identified, it is absolutely essential that data profiling be performed on the actual production data. Without data profiling, it cannot be reasonably assured that the data in question is fit for the purpose intended, nor can one have a reasonable estimate of the effort needed to develop the requested data integration solution.

Data-profiling tools will automatically perform the standard assessments and provide reports. Further analysis against the proposed source or target data can then be performed.

Data modeling

Almost certainly, central to the organization's data integration strategy is the creation of a canonical data model or common central data model providing the common format to which all the application interfaces will be transformed. This hub-and-spoke technique can change the data integration problem from an exponential function of the number of applications in the organization to a linear function, potentially making the number of interfaces a manageable problem. The interfaces and messages and views necessary for implementation of the data integration solutions all have to be modeled.

Most data-modeling tools that are used for relational data modeling may be used for the development of a canonical model, or the development tools for the integration solutions may also provide this capability.

Data flow modeling

The flow of data between the applications and organizations needs to be designed and documented for all data integration solutions in batch and real time, for both structured and unstructured data.

This capability may be available within the data integration engines, but it is also necessary to have an integrated view of the data flow across all the integration engines, interfaces, and applications.

Metadata repository

Metadata is the core of data integration solutions. It describes the structure of the sources, targets, and intermediate points, as well as the business meaning, the technical structure and transformation, and the origin of the data and how it was transformed.

Every tool and engine described above has its own metadata repository. Some but not all of these repositories can share metadata between them.

One last technology investment that should be considered in a data integration strategy is a central metadata repository that pulls all the metadata together. This can be a significant investment cost, for both the purchase and ongoing operation of an enterprise metadata repository. However, it has been demonstrated that such a repository provides an excellent way to govern data across the organization, provide both a business and technical view of the organization's data assets, and show an audit trail of data lineage suitable for regulatory reporting requirements.

The end

Data integration as an area of data management technology has tended to be somewhat neglected. This is understandable inasmuch as data integration solutions operate between areas of responsibility—that is, between applications—and so it has been difficult to identify to whom responsibility for the interfaces between applications and organizations should belong.

Without central planning for data movement and data integration in an organization, and without a data integration strategy, the organization will quickly be faced with an overwhelming and unmanageable number of interfaces. It is critically important for every organization to implement some central planning for data integration using data hubs and a canonical data model in order to be able to reasonably manage the portfolio of data interfaces between applications and other organizations.

References

Aiken, P., & Allen, D. M. (2004). *XML in data management* Burlington, MA: Morgan Kaufmann.

DAMA International (2009). *The DAMA guide to the data management body of knowledge* Bradley Beach, NJ: Technics Publications.

Ferguson, M. (2012). *Maximizing the business value of data virtualization. Enterprise data world*. Atlanta, GA.: Dataversity.

Giordano, A. D. (2011). *Data integration blueprint and modeling*. Upper Saddle River, NJ: IBM Press Pearson plc.

Inmon, W. (1996). *Building the data warehouse* (2nd ed.). New York: John Wiley & Sons.

Inmon, W., Imhoff, C., & Battas, G. (1996). *Building the operational data store*. New York: John Wiley & Sons.

Inmon, W., Imhoff, C., & Sousa, R. (1998). *The corporate information factory*. New York: John Wiley & Sons.

Inmon, W., & Krishnan, K. (2011). *Building the unstructured data warehouse*. Bradley Beach, NJ: Technics Publications, LLC.

Kimball, R., & Ross, M. (2002). *The data warehouse toolkit* (2nd ed.). New York: John Wiley & Sons.

Linthicum, D. S. (1999). *Enterprise application integration*. Addison-Wesley Professional.

Linthicum, D. S. (2003). *Next generation application integration*. Addison-Wesley Professional.

Linthicum, D. S. (2009). *Cloud computing and SOA convergence in your enterprise*. Addison-Wesley Professional.

Loshin, D. (2009). *Master data management*. Burlington, MA: Morgan Kaufmann.

Tannenbaum, A. (1994). *Implementing a corporate repository*. New York: John Wiley & Sons.

Tannenbaum, A. (2001). *Metadata solutions*. Addison-Wesley Professional.

van der Lans, R. F. (2012). *Data virtualization for business intelligence systems*. Waltham, MA: Morgan Kaufmann.

Index

Note: Page numbers followed by "*f*" and "*b*" refer to figures and boxes respectively.

Related Titles from Morgan Kaufmann

Data Virtualization for Business Intelligence Systems
Revolutionizing Data Integration for Data Warehouses
Rick F. van der Lans
9780123944252

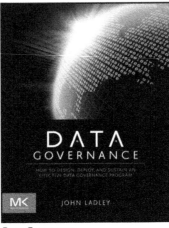

Data Governance
How to Design, Deploy, and Sustain an Effective Data Governance Program
John Ladley
9780124158290

Principles of Data Integration
Anhai Doan, Alon Halevy, Zachary Ives
9780124160446

Agile Data Warehousing Project Management
Business Intelligence Systems Using Scrum
Ralph Hughes
9780123964632

Business Intelligence, Second Edition
The Savvy Manager's Guide
David Loshin
9780123858894

Measuring Data Quality for Ongoing Improvement
A Data Quality Assessment Framework
Laura Sebastian-Coleman
9780123970336

mkp.com

Printed and bound by CPI Group (UK) Ltd, Croydon, CR0 4YY

08/06/2025

01896868-0012